SELECTED POEMS OF

BYRON

SELECTED POEMS OF
BYRON

Edited with an Introduction and Notes

by

ROBIN SKELTON

HEINEMANN
EDUCATIONAL

Heinemann Educational Books Ltd
Halley Court, Jordan Hill, Oxford OX2 8EJ

OXFORD   LONDON   EDINBURGH
MADRID   ATHENS   BOLOGNA   PARIS
MELBOURNE   SYDNEY   AUCKLAND   SINGAPORE   TOKYO
IBADAN   NAIROBI   HARARE   GABORONE
PORTSMOUTH NH (USA)

ISBN 0 435 15035 9

GEORGE GORDON, LORD BYRON, 1788—1824

INTRODUCTION AND NOTES
© ROBIN SKELTON 1964

FIRST PUBLISHED 1964
93 94 95 96 97   23 22 21 20 19 18 17 16 15 14

Printed in Great Britain by
Athenaeum Press Ltd, Newcastle upon Tyne.

CONTENTS

v

PART TWO: LONGER POEMS AND EXTRACTS

PART THREE: DON JUAN

NOTES

INDEX OF FIRST LINES

INTRODUCTION

I

THE greatest obstacle to the appreciation of Byron's poetry is Byron's life. This is not to suggest that we grow so disturbed by the chronicle of bottles and mistresses that we turn from the work in disgust, but rather that the work seems so often to depend fairly directly upon Byron's own experiences that we find ourselves wondering about the experience and not the work of art which sprang from it. Moreover, as Byron's habit was to write the greater part of his poetry in the first person, and as he continually referred to contemporaries by name, we find that the whole corpus of his work is entangled with the back-stairs gossip, the chit-chat, the political skullduggerry, the literary manœuvring, and the whole social and moral ethos of his period. This is unfortunate, in some respects. Too much has been written about Byron's Marriage, about Byron's various Love Affairs, about The Wicked Lord Byron. And yet there is very little sensible criticism of his actual verse, which is, presumably, the main reason why anyone cares to discuss Byron at all in the first place.

Of course, The Byron Story *is* a fascinating one. Born of an unhappy marriage between a dissolute Scots Peer and an emotionally overwrought heiress, in the year 1788, he was brought up in the sort of environment which would be calculated to unbalance the most phlegmatic child. His father left home in 1790, having spent almost the whole of his wife's fortune, leaving her with only a tiny annual income. His mother, of whom he was deeply fond, was given to fits of rage and near hysteria upon very slight provocation. In 1798, the ten-year-old child succeeded to the title on the death of an uncle, and he and his mother went to live at the family seat of Newstead Abbey, which was as neglected and crumbling as any Gothic novelist might wish. Byron was here, for a time, educated by his mother. He was alternately abused and coddled. In one of her fits of temper, referring to the malformed foot with which he had been born, she once called him 'a lame brat', a comment which her son never forgot, and which he thought was the cause of much of his later sensitivity upon the subject. Eventually, at his mother's suggestion, his guardian, Lord Carlisle, sent him to Harrow, where he was both pugnacious and idle. Trinity College, Cambridge, succeeded Harrow in 1805. His first collection of poems, *Fugitive Pieces,* came out in 1806; it was enlarged and republished as *Poems on Various Occasions* in 1807, and then altered yet again and issued under the title *Hours of Idleness* in the same year. This last version was the one which was reviewed by *The Edinburgh Review* in 1808. Byron was less wounded than infuriated by the reviewer's contemptuous remarks, and straightway settled down to write

> Still must I hear?—shall hoarse Fitzgerald bawl
> His creaking couplets in a tavern hall,
> And I not sing, lest, haply, Scotch reviews
> Should dub me scribbler, and denounce my muse?
> Prepare for rhyme—I'll publish, right or wrong:
> Fools are my theme, let satire be my song.

English Bards and Scotch Reviewers, a long, witty, vituperative attack upon the pretentious critics and feeble versifiers of fashionable literature of the time, was published in 1809. Byron put his name to the second edition, in which there was a frivolous snook-cocking preface, full of gaiety and aplomb. The year 1809 was also the one in which Byron came of age, and in June of that year he set off on a tour of the Mediterranean, during which he wrote the first two stanzas of *Childe Harold's Pilgrimage* and succeeded in swimming the Hellespont. He returned to England in 1811 to find his affairs in disorder. The expenses attendant upon running Newstead Abbey had put him in debt. His mother, moreover was unwell, and before he could reach her bedside at Newstead, she died. On August 7 Byron wrote to Scrope Davies: 'Some curse hangs over me and mine. My mother lies a corpse in this house; one of my best friends is drowned in a ditch. What can I say, or think, or do?'

He did all that he could, selling those verses that he had already written, and settling down to write more. *Childe Harold's Pilgrimage* and *The Curse of Minerva* appeared in 1812, *The Waltz* in 1813, and in 1813 also *The Giaour* appeared, and ran to eight editions within the year. Byron was now a famous man. *Childe Harold* had made him famous overnight, and the hectic romantic adventure stories of *The Giaour*, *The Bride of Abydos* (1813), *The Corsair* (1814), *Lara* (1814), together with many shorter poems, appealed greatly to the public. It is not very surprising that Byron should enjoy success in the way he did. He was, after all, a young man in his early twenties, courted and flattered by almost everyone, and no prude. It has been suggested that he suffered from an inferiority complex which derived from his self-consciousness about his lame foot, and that his many love affairs were all attempts to prove to himself how attractive and virile he was. This may or may not be true, but certainly Byron spent a good deal of energy pursuing and being pursued by young women, some of whom led him into passionate entanglements and almost comical emotional complications.

He viewed all these matters (if we are to rely upon his letters) with a very healthy (some might say cynical) detachment. His letters to the ladies concerned may breathe passionate sighs, as is proper, but his tone to his friends and confidants is often less sentimental. This is, after all, quite usual. There is no need to accuse Byron of extreme wickedness, though one could certainly convict him of an almost heroic lack of discretion. No one knows exactly why Byron's marriage to Miss Millbanks failed. They were married in 1815, and shortly after the birth of a daughter almost twelve months later, the marriage broke up. Lady Byron left her husband without any satisfactory explanation. Rumours were numerous and all to Byron's discredit; so violently did people feel about their fallen idol that eventually Byron felt obliged to leave the country, never to return again.

Byron spent the remaining years of his life very largely in Italy, where he wrote, drank, and made love with his usual zest. His last mistress, Teresa Guiccioli, a temperamental young woman with a broadminded husband, later regarded herself as his One True Love, but as her versions of her relationship with the poet varied over the years, this is not, perhaps, reliable evidence. It was Byron's hatred of oppression and love of liberty which brought him to his death, however, and not his rakish excesses. He supported the Greeks in their revolt against their Turkish masters, and in 1824 he joined their army, and showed himself to be as full of inventiveness, energy, and decisiveness in martial as in literary and amorous matters. Unfortunately, however, he fell ill of a fever at Missolonghi and died there on April 19, 1824, leaving a personal legend so richly interesting, so full of ambiguous situations, and so adorned by rumour, that people have been investigating The Truth About Lord Byron ever since.

His death was an occasion, says one commentator, for 'the sorrow of all civilized Europe'; it must, however, have also been a source of considerable relief to a number of private individuals. It was, most certainly, a cause for true sorrow in Greece, one of whose National Heroes he became at that moment. His friends, too, who received his wildly exuberant letters, and who loved him for his vitality, candour, and generosity of heart, mourned him without affectation. The rest of the world settled down to talk about him. And, for all the time that has passed since his death, no one has yet attempted to study and evaluate the poetry without relating it to the personality. There is some justice in this for perhaps Byron's greatest contribution to English Letters was his legend rather than his verses. What does, however, happen when one pushes the portrait of that handsomest of poets aside, and starts reading some selection of the best of his verses?

4

It is not easy to push the legend aside, for Byron's poems are often dramatic monologues, which are concerned to interest us as much in the character as in the statements of the speaker, and that speaker is often rather like the man in the portrait we are trying to discard. Indeed, Byron used a good deal of autobiographical material in his poetry, being, at least in this respect, in agreement with Wordsworth over the importance of studying recollected emotion. Just as Wordsworth's self-portrait in *The Prelude* (or in many of his shorter poems) differs markedly from the Wordsworth we have described to us by his contemporaries, so the Byron of *Childe Harold* differs from the Byron of his letters or of his friends' reports. The hero of *Childe Harold* is a gloomy, overwrought young man, bitter, handsome, and solitary. His wild soul is troubled by dreams of social justice; his sad eye kindles at the magnificence of all the more turbulent forms of scenery. Learned, he is no pedant, but sufficient of a scholar and a gentleman to be moved by antiquities, and to be able to reflect in an informed manner upon the glories of the past and the comparative decadence of the present. He travels through various countries, making political and æsthetic comments, but his real interest is in his own sorrow and despair—neither of which are ever quite defined in his numerous references to them.

Byron, on the other hand, seems rather to have enjoyed his European tour, and if he was racked by a secret sorrow, he keeps it pretty well concealed in his letters, though there are occasional references to his dislike of England, and his comparative friendlessness. It is, indeed, wise to see the hero of *Childe Harold*, not as a self-portrait by Byron, but as Byron's first shot at creating a hero who could serve as the narrator of a long poem, which should reflect generally upon men and manners, and which should have, as part of its interest for the reader, the quality of being in some way a gradual exploration of the speaker's own character. Thus our belief in the statements made, and our trust in the opinions expressed, must be qualified by our attitude towards the speaker. Moreover, in *Childe Harold* (as later and magnificently in *Don Juan*), the speaker is not given the rather cypher-like urbanity of a professional observer, but is provided with fancies, prejudices, and passions in profusion. Thus, we are required to make, while reading the poem, a continual series of adjustments, emotional and intellectual, to the speaker, even while also reacting to the speaker's statements; this means that the poem promotes a richer and more satisfying response in the reader, than if it were simply to direct us to take the narrator on trust.

This method of writing is not, of course, an innovation by Byron. Chaucer used it in *The Canterbury Tales*, after all. John Donne used it in his Elegies. Many of the Cavalier Poets used it in quite short lyrics. Pope makes great use of it in the *Epistle to Arbuthnot*. Cowper's *Task* is based upon it. The novel, too, uses this structure. We can see the method in use if we look at Defoe or Richardson, or (after Byron's time) Emily Brontë, Dickens, Wilkie Collins (who used multiple first person narrators), or Henry James. In poetry after Byron it reaches its highpoint in Browning's *The Ring and The Book*, and his example affected the work of Edward Thomas, Robert Frost, and T. S. Eliot (to mention only a few). I make this digression to show that, whereas there was a fashion in Byron's time for the poetical autobiography, there was also an established tradition of the dramatic monologue in which the speaker was not entirely to be trusted by the perceptive reader. It is therefore unwise to assume that *Childe Harold* was as closely related to Byron as many critics seem to think. Byron, like many novelists, built his first considerable poem with the material that lay first to hand—fragments of his own experience—that is all. *Childe Harold* came out of Byron's European tour, but it is not in any serious way an account of it.

Byron is, indeed, more of a writer of fiction than many poets. Although his work includes several magnificently personal poems, it also contains such novelettes in verse as *The Prisoner of Chillon*,

The Siege of Corinth, and *The Corsair*. Stories in verse were not unusual at this time, of course. Many eighteenth-century poets had written fables. The interest in narrative ballads had been intense for a great many years. Among the Romantic Poets, Southey was as interested in creating melodramatic, highly coloured, narratives of passion as was Byron. Coleridge had his *Ancient Mariner* and *Christabel*. Wordsworth, less concerned with the bizarre and violent, nevertheless touches on this area in several poems. We cannot, therefore, call Byron original simply because he wrote such stories; we may rightly call his manner of writing them original.

One of the original aspects of Byron's tales is their refusal to indulge in any philosophizing that is not a part of the story. The story is the thing, and it moves along rapidly, without ever allowing the reader to become bored. Any reflective passages are built firmly into the plot, and made as lively as much of the action. Thus in *Mazeppa* we get:

> The sun was sinking—still I lay
> Chain'd to the chill and stiffening steed·
> I thought to mingle there our clay
>   And my dim eyes of death had need;
>   No hope arose of being freed:
> I cast my last looks up the sky,
>   And there between me and the sun
> I saw the expecting raven fly,
> Who scarce would wait till both should die,
>   Ere his repast begun;
> He flew, and perch'd, then flew once more,
> And each time nearer than before;
> I saw his wing through twilight flit,
> And once so near me he alit
>   I could have smote, but lack'd the strength;
> But the slight motion of my hand,
> And feeble scratchings of the sand,
> The exerted throat's faint struggling noise,
> Which scarcely could be called a voice,
>   Together scared him off at length.

7

I know no more—my latest dream
  Is something of a lovely star
  Which fix'd my dull eye from afar,
And went and came with wandering beam,
And all the cold, dull, swimming, dense
Sensation of recurring sense,
And then subsiding back to death,
And then again a little breath,
A little thrill, a short suspense,
  An icy sickness curdling o'er
My heart, and sparks that cross'd my brain—
A gasp, a throb, a start of pain,
  A sigh, and nothing more.

This section begins with an expression of the speaker's thoughts, and then moves on to picture his thoughts and feelings more clearly, and in terms of his actions and the scene as a whole. Byron has this magnificent ability to keep his poems concrete; abstract philosophizing is almost always supported by particular images, definite references. The world of Byron's poems is intensely sensual; no thought can escape for long its essential dependence upon the physical world.

This passage from *Mazeppa* also illustrates another Byron characteristic. The stories he chose to tell were most frequently of love and suffering, and often involved violence. The hero is a man possessed by a secret sorrow, a secret guilt; he stands apart from his fellows and broods. The landscapes are either incredibly lush and beautiful, or monstrously craggy and arid. The heroines remind one in their physical perfection of some of the photographs of today's film stars. Indeed, one might well think of Byron's narratives as being relations of those of Hollywood. Byron's *The Island* is his version of *The Mutiny on the Bounty*, and in its constant attention to visual detail, as well as in its rather crudely effective character portraits, is very reminiscent of a cinematic treatment.

It might be thought that to compare Byron with Hollywood is to insult him, but, in fact, Byron was much more concerned with the rôle of the poet as entertainer than we normally suppose. He may have important things to say, and passionate stories to tell, but he also has an audience to captivate, and of this he is never unaware. As one reads through any long poem of Byron's, it is easy to see the way that he keeps his poem lively by altering the tone. Often, there will be a touch of light relief after a sombre passage; sometimes it feels as if the story-teller is deliberately poking sly fun at himself by making his descriptions a little over-colourful; often there are digressions which the story-teller apologizes for —much as the story-teller in Chaucer's *The Nonnes Preestes Tale* digresses and apologizes. This concern of Byron's to entertain may spring partly from his need as a professional writer to sell his wares; it may also stem from his wishing to counteract his feeling of social rejection by gaining popularity as a poet: it is, however, just as likely that Byron's view of the poet's task was less pretentious, and, in some ways, more traditional than that of his fellows. Although in his earliest poems he adopted a tone of voice which suggested that the poet was a significant person in so far as he was able to express the passionate depths of the human heart, in his later poems it seems that the poet is regarded less as a prophet and martyr than as a story-teller and as a dramatist.

Of course, there is a great deal of variety in Byron's work, and he has occasionally been blamed for his range of manner. Consequently any generalization about his view of the poet's rôle will be false, unless it takes this variety into account. Byron composed plays, satires, epigrams, lyrics, adventure stories, eclogues, and verse translations. His tone of voice ranges from the crudest vernacular to the most sublime rhetoric. His poems include private occasional poems, and public political utterances. What possible formula can cover all this?

The answer is straightforward. Byron's concept of the poet's task grew, after his earliest work, to be one closely related to an eighteenth-century attitude. Worshipping Alexander Pope, as he did, Byron clearly felt that a poet should not adopt too many grandiose airs, but should see his task as both entertainment and instruction. He should concern himself less with the idea of the poet as a seer, than with the notion of the poet as observer and moralist. Nevertheless, there was a proper place for the sublime in narratives of great men taking part in great actions. In such stories there should be implicit, if not explicit, a moral teaching, and the manner of the tale should be appropriately grand. In addition to this, the poet could legitimately, if he wished, indulge in jokes and lampoons. He should also, like the poets in the Greek Anthology, compose epitaphs—both of a serious and a satiric kind. A poet is not a man possessed by divine inspiration sc much as a craftsman whose sensibility and wit enable him to deligh·, instruct, and castigate, the society of which he is a part.

Byron, taking this view of the poet, and feeling also that the Wordsworthian and Coleridgean attitudes were pretentious and obscurantist, frequently chattered of his work as if he were without any real feeling for it; he talked as if the writing of poetry came to him as easily as the scribbling of his long amusing letters. Nevertheless we know that Byron's poems were written with great care, and often revised; his pose of careless facility was a pose only, and once calculated to enrage any too earnest follower of the Lakeland poets. This pose places Byron not only alongside many writers of the eighteenth century, but also alongside Carew and the Cavaliers of the seventeenth century, whom Pope once dismissed as 'that mob of gentlemen that writ with ease'. It was Carew's aim to sound as if his verse had been dashed off spontaneously; again, however, we know that he burned midnight oil over most of his poems. The word 'gentlemen' is interesting here. Pope saw that the Cavaliers' pose was a social attitude; it implied superiority. It also implied authority. A gentleman, by breeding and education, had the right to make his urbane comments upon the social scene.

Byron, though a democrat by political conviction, nevertheless adopted this gentlemanly tone in many of his poems, and in particular in *Don Juan*. Thus we have in the one poetic personality the journeyman entertainer, the poet who knows what a poet's rôle is, and the brilliant amateur who dabbles in writing. Again, one is forced to the conclusion that the Byronic Gentleman of *Don Juan*, the witty and carelessly brilliant narrator, is as much of a fictional creation as the gloomy hero of *Childe Harold*, and that Byron's overall view of the poet's task includes the view that a part of his rôle is the impersonation of significant characters. Some of these may pretend to the name Byron and some may not, but all are created for a purpose.

The purpose of the narrators in *The Giaour,* or *The Island,* or *The Prisoner of Chillon* is easy enough to see: they are the tellers of tales, and their job is simply to enthral. The speaker of *The Vision of Judgment,* or of *Childe Harold* has a character which enables him to discuss what he wishes from a particular and prejudiced point of view. The speaker of *Don Juan* is, of all Byron's creations, the most complex, and the most brilliantly successful. In his person Byron answers his main problem, which was to create a speaker who could, while being immensely sensitive to natural beauty, and to matters of emotion, also take up a worldly and cynical attitude towards much of the world about him. He must be a man who is fully aware of his status as an entertainer and raconteur, and yet also a man who has strong convictions and beliefs which he will not gloss over in order to please. He must have all the social graces to enable him to speak with authority of high society; but he must also have enough individuality and rebelliousness to allow him to be vulgar from time to time without risk of being thought either affected or ill-bred. He must appear superior to his audience and seem careless of its views, even while he endeavours to be entertaining: he must, in a word, be the perfect talker. And he must give the impression that he can talk about everything.

Byron's creation of this figure is one of the great landmarks in English Literature. There have been other great narrators invented —the narrator of *Tristram Shandy* is one that is like the narrator of *Don Juan* in being perpetually digressive and frequently risqué, and the narrators of Charles Churchill's long amusing poems have all a cousinly resemblance to Byron's creation. Byron took his manner, however, and therefore a good part of the character of his speaker from a poem by John Hookham Frere, written under the pseudonym of 'William and Robert Whistlecraft', of which four cantos appeared in 1817–1818. This is a poem which states at the outset that it is built upon a new plan—which is to have no plan at all and wander where chance wills. The verse form used is also that used by Byron for *Don Juan*, and the facetiousness of the brothers Whistlecraft is much of the same kind.

Byron did not, therefore, invent the shape of *Don Juan* without help. Indeed, Byron is less an innovator than an inheritor; he takes much that other writers have bequeathed him, and develops it farther. He is thus much less of a true revolutionary than Wordsworth, who attempted to create a totally new stance for the poet to adopt. He is, likewise, more conventional than either Shelley or Keats. Nevertheless, the effect of his developing already accepted conventions is quite as startling as the innovations of his contemporaries. No one before Byron ever managed to get into one poem two such different tones of voice as in:

> Her glossy hair was cluster'd o'er a brow
>> Bright with intelligence, and fair, and smooth;
> Her eyebrow's shape was like the aërial bow,
>> Her cheek all purple with the beam of youth,
> Mounting, at times to a transparent glow,
>> As if her veins ran lightning; she, in sooth,
> Possess'd an air and grace by no means common:
>> Her stature tall—I hate a dumpy woman.

Here, after an apparently rapturous description, we get an anticlimax, and the sort of commonplace remark that brings us down to earth with a jerk. Byron is always doing this—leading us up the garden path, teasing us, surprising us with comedy when we expect high seriousness. This teaches us to be aware of our own foolish credulity; it teaches us scepticism, and it questions the depth of emotions that are so easily roused and then so easily destroyed. Byron also indulges himself in jokes at his own expense, in outrageous rhymes, even in passages of near nonsense.

12

Barnave, Brissot, Condorcet, Mirabeau,
    Pétion, Clootz, Danton, Marat, La Fayette,
Were French, and famous people, as we know;
    And there were others scarce forgotten yet,
Joubert, Hoche, Marceau, Lannes, Desaix, Moreau,
    With many of the military set,
Exceedingly remarkable at times,
But not at all adapted to my rhymes.

This is simply a gay piece of showing-off. It makes it clear that the
poem in which such things can occur has absolute freedom of
movement. It can say or do almost anything, and *Don Juan* lives
up to this possibility. Over its sixteen cantos it deals with subjects
ranging from politics to hangovers, and with places from London
to Turkey and back. It deals with man in his most private as in
his most public moments. It ranges in tone from the vulgar to the
sublime, from the outrageously farcical to the poignantly heroic.
It contains within it, one is tempted to say, one of the finest full-
length portraits of humanity ever conceived, and it places Byron,
for his wit and human understanding, alongside Cervantes and
Balzac. Indeed, in its shape, it owes something to the picaresque
novel of which Cervantes was the father; it is much more close
to Fielding's *Tom Jones* in structure than it is to any preceding
poetry. Like Fielding, Byron creates a hero who shall suffer many
adventures, during which he will prove his attractiveness to the
opposite sex, his lack of a more than rudimentary moral sense, and
his fine capacity for making the best of things. This hero will
provide the excuse for reflections and digressions upon many
topics, some serious, some not: he will move through different
strata of society and let us observe differences of manners. Don
Juan, like Tom Jones, like Swift's Gulliver, like Bunyan's Christian,
is the excuse for a survey of man's condition that shall be both
entertaining and instructive.

Byron has been neglected by many critics, and by many readers,
because he does not fit comfortably into our picture of the Romantic
Revolution led by Wordsworth and Coleridge, followed through

by Keats and Shelley, and consolidated by Tennyson. He is, in his resolute intelligence, closer to the uncomfortably observant Browning than to the introspective Keats. His opinions, too, fit none of the tidy patterns. A radical, he abuses many liberal thinkers. An aristocrat, he objects continually to the feudal and tyrannical. Moreover, his enthusiasms are often not particularly respectable. He enjoys wine, women, and song, and says so with hearty candour. He cannot easily be fitted alongside those of his contemporaries who so consistently appeared to reverence the notion of female purity. Byron's heroines are admired for their beauty, good sense, and candour, rather than for their chastity.

Byron is an uncomfortable sort of poet for this reason, and yet he is in many ways a more 'modern' poet than his contemporaries —that is to say, he seems to be closer to the second half of the twentieth century. Like so many of our living writers, he combines political idealism with social scepticism: he has faith in ideals of liberty and fraternity, but little faith in their political representatives. Like many of our writers, he is suspicious of the heroic gesture, even while he feels moved by it; he cannot, at the end, commit himself wholeheartedly to anything but detestation of the tyrannies and cant of the 'Establishment'. *Don Juan* is one of the great forerunners of the poetry of irony and social criticism, of scepticism and anger, which fills so many pages today. It is not an accident that W. H. Auden wrote a *Letter to Lord Byron* in which he suggested that they had rôles in common. Byron, story-teller and entertainer, believer in tradition, invented, in *Don Juan*, much of the poetry of our own time.

PART ONE

SHORTER POEMS

I would I were a Careless Child

I would I were a careless child,
  Still dwelling in my Highland cave,
Or roaming through the dusky wild,
  Or bounding o'er the dark blue wave;
The cumbrous pomp of Saxon pride
  Accords not with the freeborn soul,
Which loves the mountain's craggy side,
  And seeks the rocks where billows roll.

Fortune! take back these cultured lands,
  Take back this name of splendid sound!   10
I hate the touch of servile hands,
  I hate the slaves that cringe around.
Place me among the rocks I love,
  Which sound to Ocean's wildest roar;
I ask but this—again to rove
  Through scenes my youth hath known before.

Few are my years, and yet I feel
  The world was ne'er design'd for me:
Ah! why do dark'ning shades conceal
  The hour when man must cease to be?   20
Once I beheld a splendid dream,
  A visionary scene of bliss:
Truth!—wherefore did thy hated beam
  Awake me to a world like this?

I loved—but those I loved are gone;
  Had friends—my early friends are fled:
How cheerless feels the heart alone,
  When all its former hopes are dead!
Though gay companions o'er the bowl
  Dispel awhile the sense of ill;   30
  Though pleasure stirs the maddening soul,
    The heart—the heart—is lonely still.

How dull! to hear the voice of those
  Whom rank or chance, whom wealth or power,
Have made, though neither friends nor foes,
  Associates of the festive hour.
Give me again a faithful few,
  In years and feelings still the same,
And I will fly the midnight crew,
  Where boist'rous joy is but a name.   40

And woman, lovely woman! thou,
  My hope, my comforter, my all!
How cold must be my bosom now,
  When e'en thy smiles begin to pall!
Without a sigh would I resign
  This busy scene of splendid woe,
To make that calm contentment mine,
  Which virtue knows, or seems to know.

Fain would I fly the haunts of men—
  I seek to shun, not hate mankind;   50
My breast requires the sullen glen,
  Whose gloom may suit a darken'd mind.
Oh! that to me the wings were given
  Which bear the turtle to her nest!
Then would I cleave the vault of heaven,
  To flee away, and be at rest.

From Anacreon

[Μεσονυκτίαις ποθ' ὥραις, κ. τ. λ.]

'Twas now the hour when Night had driven
Her car half round yon sable heaven;
Boötes, only, seem'd to roll
His arctic charge around the pole;
While mortals, lost in gentle sleep,
Forgot to smile, or ceased to weep:
At this lone hour the Paphian boy,
Descending from the realms of joy,
Quick to my gate directs his course,
And knocks with all his little force.   10
My visions fled, alarm'd I rose,—
'What stranger breaks my blest repose?'
'Alas!' replies the wily child,
In faltering accents sweetly mild,
'A hapless infant here I roam,
Far from my dear maternal home.
Oh! shield me from the wintry blast!
The nightly storm is pouring fast.
No prowling robber fingers here.
A wandering baby who can fear?'   20
I heard his seeming artless tale,
I heard his sighs upon the gale:
My breast was never pity's foe,
But felt for all the baby's woe.
I drew the bar, and by the light
Young Love, the infant, met my sight;
His bow across his shoulders flung,
And thence his fatal quiver hung

17

(Ah! little did I think the dart
Would rankle soon within my heart). 30
With care I tend my weary guest,
His little fingers chill my breast;
His glossy curls, his azure wing,
Which droop with nightly showers, I wring;
His shivering limbs the embers warm;
And now reviving from the storm,
Scarce had he felt his wonted glow,
Than swift he seized his slender bow:—
'I fain would know, my gentle host,'
He cried, 'if this its strength has lost; 40
I fear, relax'd with midnight dews,
The strings their former aid refuse.'
With poison tipt, his arrow flies,
Deep in my tortured heart it lies:
Then loud the joyous urchin laugh'd:—
'My bow can still impel the shaft:
'Tis firmly fix'd, thy sighs reveal it;
Say, courteous host, canst thou not feel it?'

To the Author of a Sonnet

Beginning ' "Sad is my verse", you say, " and yet no tear"'

Thy verse is 'sad' enough, no doubt:
    A devilish deal more sad than witty!
Why we should weep I can't find out,
    Unless for *thee* we weep in pity.

Yet there is one I pity more;
    And much, alas! I think he needs it;

18

For he, I'm sure, will suffer sore,
   Who, to his own misfortune, reads it.

Thy rhymes, without the aid of magic,
   May *once* be read—but never after: 10
Yet their effect's by no means tragic,
   Although by far too dull for laughter.

But would you make our bosoms bleed,
   And of no common pang complain—
If you would make us weep indeed,
   Tell us, you'll read them o'er again.

Farewell! If Ever Fondest Prayer

Farewell! if ever fondest prayer
   For other's weal avail'd on high,
Mine will not all be lost in air,
   But waft thy name beyond the sky.
'Twere vain to speak, to weep, to sigh:
   Oh! more than tears of blood can tell,
When wrung from guilt's expiring eye,
   Are in that word—Farewell!—Farewell!

These lips are mute, these eyes are dry;
   But in my breast and in my brain,   10
Awake the pangs that pass not by,
   The thought that ne'er shall sleep again.
My soul nor deigns nor dares complain,
   Though grief and passion there rebel;
I only know we loved in vain—
   I only feel—Farewell!—Farewell!

Remember Thee! Remember Thee!

Remember thee! remember thee!
    Till Lethe quench life's burning stream
Remorse and shame shall cling to thee,
    And haunt thee like a feverish dream!

Remember thee! Ay, doubt it not.
    Thy husband too shall think of thee!
By neither shalt thou be forgot,
    Thou *false* to him, thou *fiend* to me!

Written after Swimming from Sestos to Abydos

If, in the month of dark December,
    Leander, who was nightly wont
(What maid will not the tale remember?)
    To cross thy stream, broad Hellespont!

If, when the wintry tempest roar'd,
    He sped to Hero, nothing loth,
And thus of old thy current pour'd,
    Fair Venus! how I pity both!

For *me*, degenerate modern wretch,
    Though in the genial month of May,   10
My dripping limbs I faintly stretch,
    And think I've done a feat to-day.

But since he cross'd the rapid tide,
    According to the doubtful story,
To woo,—and—Lord knows what beside,
    And swam for Love, as I for Glory;

'Twere hard to say who fared the best:
   Sad mortals! thus the gods still plague you!
He lost his labour, I my jest;
   For he was drown'd, and I've the ague.   20

The Spell is Broke, the Charm is Flown!

Written at Athens, January 16, 1810

The spell is broke, the charm is flown!
   Thus is it with life's fitful fever:
We madly smile when we should groan:
   Delirium is our best deceiver.

Each lucid interval of thought
   Recalls the woes of Nature's charter;
And he that acts as wise men ought,
   But lives, as saints have died, a martyr.

To Belshazzar

Belshazzar! from the banquet turn,
   Nor in thy sensual fulness fall;
Behold! while yet before thee burn
   The graven words, the glowing wall,
Many a despot men miscall
   Crown'd and anointed from on high;
But thou, the weakest, worst of all—
   Is it not written, thou must die?

21

Go! dash the roses from thy brow—
  Grey hairs but poorly wreathe with them;   10
Youth's garlands misbecome thee now,
  More than thy very diadem,
Where thou hast tarnish'd every gem:—
  Then throw the worthless bauble by,
Which, worn by thee, ev'n slaves contemn;
  And learn like better men to die!

Oh! early in the balance weigh'd,
  And ever light of word and worth,
Whose soul expired ere youth decay'd,
  And left thee but a mass of earth.   20
To see thee moves the scorner's mirth:
  But tears in Hope's averted eye
Lament that even thou hadst birth—
  Unfit to govern, live, or die.

To Thomas Moore

I

My boat is on the shore,
  And my bark is on the sea;
But, before I go, Tom Moore,
  Here's a double health to thee!

II

Here's a sigh to those who love me,
  And a smile to those who hate;
And, whatever sky's above me,
  Here's a heart for every fate.

III

Though the ocean roar around me,
  Yet it still shall bear me on;
Though a desert should surround me,
  It hath springs that may be won.

10

IV

Were't the last drop in the well,
  As I gasp'd upon the brink,
Ere my fainting spirit fell,
  'Tis to thee that I would drink.

V

With that water, as this wine,
  The libation I would pour
Should be—peace with thine and mine,
  And a health to thee, Tom Moore.

20

So, We'll Go No More a Roving

I

So, we'll go no more a roving
  So late into the night,
Though the heart be still as loving,
  And the moon be still as bright.

II

For the sword outwears its sheath,
  And the soul wears out the breast,
And the heart must pause to breathe,
  And love itself have rest.

23

III

Though the night was made for loving,
  And the day returns too soon,
Yet we'll go no more a roving
  By the light of the moon.

Four Epigrams

I

The world is a bundle of hay,
  Mankind are the asses who pull;
Each tugs it a different way,
  And the greatest of all is John Bull.

II

So Castlereagh has cut his throat!—The worst
Of this is,—that his own was not the first.

EPIGRAM ON MY WEDDING-DAY

TO PENELOPE

This day, of all our days, has done
  The worst for me and you:—
'Tis just *six* years since we were *one*,
  And *five* since we were *two*.

ON MY THIRTY-THIRD BIRTHDAY

JANUARY 22, 1821

Through life's dull road, so dim and dirty,
I have dragg'd to three-and-thirty.
What have these years left to me?
Nothing—except thirty-three.

Darkness

I had a dream, which was not all a dream.
The bright sun was extinguish'd, and the stars
Did wander darkling in the eternal space,
Rayless, and pathless, and the icy earth
Swung blind and blackening in the moonless air;
Morn came and went—and came, and brought no day,
And men forgot their passions in the dread
Of this their desolation; and all hearts
Were chill'd into a selfish prayer for light:
And they did live by watchfires—and the thrones,   10
The palaces of crowned kings—the huts,
The habitations of all things which dwell,
Were burnt for beacons; cities were consumed,
And men were gather'd round their blazing homes
To look once more into each other's face;
Happy were those who dwelt within the eye
Of the volcanos, and their mountain-torch:
A fearful hope was all the world contain'd;
Forests were set on fire—but hour by hour
They fell and faded—and the crackling trunks   20
Extinguish'd with a crash—and all was black.
The brows of men by the despairing light
Wore an unearthly aspect, as by fits
The flashes fell upon them; some lay down
And hid their eyes and wept; and some did rest
Their chins upon their clenched hands, and smiled;
And others hurried to and fro, and fed
Their funeral piles with fuel, and look'd up
With mad disquietude on the dull sky,

The pall of a past world; and then again 30
With curses cast them down upon the dust,
And gnash'd their teeth and howl'd: the wild birds shriek'd
And, terrified, did flutter on the ground,
And flap their useless wings; the wildest brutes
Came tame and tremulous; and vipers crawl'd
And twined themselves among the multitude,
Hissing, but stingless—they were slain for food.
And War, which for a moment was no more,
Did glut himself again:—a meal was bought
With blood, and each sate sullenly apart 40
Gorging himself in gloom: no love was left;
All earth was but one thought—and that was death
Immediate and inglorious; and the pang
Of famine fed upon all entrails—men
Died, and their bones were tombless as their flesh;
The meagre by the meagre were devour'd,
Even dogs assail'd their masters, all save one,
And he was faithful to a corse, and kept
The birds and beasts and famish'd men at bay,
Till hunger clung them, or the dropping dead 50
Lured their lank jaws; himself sought out no food,
But with a piteous and perpetual moan,
And a quick desolate cry, licking the hand
Which answer'd not with a caress—he died.
The crowd was famish'd by degrees; but two
Of an enormous city did survive,
And they were enemies: they met beside
The dying embers of an altar-place
Where had been heap'd a mass of holy things
For an unholy usage; they raked up, 60
And shivering scraped with their cold skeleton hands
The feeble ashes, and their feeble breath
Blew for a little life, and made a flame
Which was a mockery; then they lifted up

Their eyes as it grew lighter, and beheld
Each other's aspects—saw, and shriek'd, and died—
Even of their mutual hideousness they died,
Unknowing who he was upon whose brow
Famine had written Fiend. The world was void,
The populous and the powerful was a lump,   70
Seasonless, herbless, treeless, manless, lifeless,
A lump of death—a chaos of hard clay.
The rivers, lakes, and ocean all stood still,
And nothing stirr'd within their silent depths;
Ships sailorless lay rotting on the sea,
And their masts fell down piecemeal: as they dropp'd
They slept on the abyss without a surge—
The waves were dead; the tides were in their grave,
The moon, their mistress, had expired before;
The winds were wither'd in the stagnant air,   80
And the clouds perish'd; Darkness had no need
Of aid from them—She was the Universe.

She Walks in Beauty

I

She walks in beauty, like the night
  Of cloudless climes and starry skies;
And all that's best of dark and bright
  Meet in her aspect and her eyes:
Thus mellow'd to that tender light
  Which heaven to gaudy day denies.

II

One shade, the more, one ray the less,
  Had half impair'd the nameless grace
Which waves in every raven tress,

Or softly lightens o'er her face; <10>10</10>
Where thoughts serenely sweet express
  How pure, how dear their dwelling-place.

III

And on that cheek, and o'er that brow,
  So soft, so calm, yet eloquent,
The smiles that win, the tints that glow,
  But tell of days in goodness spent,
A mind at peace with all below,
  A heart whose love is innocent!

When Coldness Wraps this Suffering Clay

I

When coldness wraps this suffering clay,
  Ah! whither strays the immortal mind?
It cannot die, it cannot stay,
  But leaves its darken'd dust behind.
Then, unembodied, doth it trace
  By steps each planet's heavenly way?
Or fill at once the realms of space,
  A thing of eyes, that all survey?

II

Eternal, boundless, undecay'd,
  A thought unseen, but seeing all, <10>10</10>
All, all in earth or skies display'd,
  Shall it survey, shall it recall:
Each fainter trace that memory holds
  So darkly of departed years,
In one broad glance the soul beholds,
  And all, that was, at once appears.

III

Before Creation peopled earth,
   Its eye shall roll through chaos back;
And where the furthest heaven had birth,
   The spirit trace its rising track.   20
And where the future mars or makes,
   Its glance dilate o'er all to be,
While sun is quench'd or system breaks,
   Fix'd in its own eternity.

IV

Above or Love, Hope, Hate, or Fear,
   It lives all passionless and pure:
An age shall fleet like earthly year;
   Its years as moments shall endure.
Away, away, without a wing,
   O'er all, through all, its thought shall fly,   30
A nameless and eternal thing,
   Forgetting what it was to die.

One Struggle More, and I am Free

One struggle more, and I am free
   From pangs that rend my heart in twain;
One last long sigh to love and thee,
   Then back to busy life again.
It suits me well to mingle now
   With things that never pleased before!
Though every joy is fled below,
   What future grief can touch me more?

Then bring me wine, the banquet bring;
   Man was not form'd to live alone: 10
I'll be that light, unmeaning thing
   That smiles with all, and weeps with none.
It was not thus in days more dear,
   It never would have been, but thou
Hast fled, and left me lonely here;
   Thou'rt nothing—all are nothing now.

In vain my lyre would lightly breathe!
   The smile that sorrow fain would wear
But mocks the woe that lurks beneath,
   Like roses o'er a sepulchre.   20
Though gay companions o'er the bowl
   Dispel awhile the sense of ill:
Though pleasure fires the maddening soul,
   The heart—the heart is lonely still!

On many a lone and lovely night
   It sooth'd to gaze upon the sky;
For then I deem'd the heavenly light
   Shone sweetly on thy pensive eye:
And oft I thought at Cynthia's noon,
   When sailing o'er the Ægean wave,   30
'Now Thyrza gazes on that moon'—
   Alas, it gleam'd upon her grave!

When stretch'd on fever's sleepless bed,
   And sickness shrunk my throbbing veins,
''Tis comfort still,' I faintly said,
   'That Thyrza cannot know my pains:'
Like freedom to the time-worn slave,
   A boon 'tis idle then to give,
Relenting Nature vainly gave
   My life, when Thyrza ceased to live!   40

My Thyrza's pledge in better days,
    When love and life alike were new!
How different now thou meet'st my gaze!
    How tinged by time with sorrow's hue!
The heart that gave itself with thee
    Is silent—ah, were mine as still!
Though cold as e'en the dead can be,
    It feels, it sickens with the chill.

Thou bitter pledge! thou mournful token!
    Though painful, welcome to my breast!   50
Still, still preserve that love unbroken,
    Or break the heart to which thou'rt press'd.
Time tempers love, but not removes,
    More hallow'd when its hope is fled:
Oh! what are thousand living loves
    To that which cannot quit the dead?

The Destruction of Sennacherib

I

The Assyrian came down like the wolf on the fold,
And his cohorts were gleaming in purple and gold;
And the sheen of their spears was like stars on the sea,
When the blue wave rolls nightly on deep Galilee.

II

Like the leaves of the forest when Summer is green,
That host with their banners at sunset were seen:
Like the leaves of the forest when Autumn hath blown,
That host on the morrow lay wither'd and strown.

III

For the Angel of Death spread his wings on the blast,
And breathed in the face of the foe as he pass'd;   10
And the eyes of the sleepers wax'd deadly and chill,
And their hearts but once heaved, and for ever grew still!

IV

And there lay the steed with his nostril all wide,
But through it there roll'd not the breath of his pride;
And the foam of his gasping lay white on the turf,
And cold as the spray of the rock-beating surf.

V

And there lay the rider distorted and pale,
With the dew on his brow, and the rust on his mail:
And the tents were all silent, the banners alone,
The lances unlifted, the trumpet unblown.   20

VI

And the widows of Ashur are loud in their wail,
And the idols are broke in the temple of Baal;
And the might of the Gentile, unsmote by the sword,
Hath melted like snow in the glance of the Lord!

From

The Corsair

XXI

He ask'd no question—all were answer'd now
By the first glance on that still, marble brow.
It was enough—she died—what reck'd it how?
The love of youth, the hope of better years,
The source of softest wishes, tenderest fears,
The only living thing he could not hate,

Was reft at once—and he deserved his fate,
But did not feel it less;—the good explore,
For peace, those realms where guilt can never soar:
The proud, the wayward—who have fix'd below   10
Their joy, and find this earth enough for woe,
Lose in that one their all—perchance a mite—
But who in patience parts with all delight?
Full many a stoic eye and aspect stern
Mask hearts where grief hath little left to learn;
And many a withering thought lies hid, not lost,
In smiles that least befit who wear them most.

XXII

By those, that deepest feel, is ill exprest
The indistinctness of the suffering breast;
Where thousand thoughts begin to end in one,   20
Which seeks from all the refuge found in none;
No words suffice the secret soul to show,
For Truth denies all eloquence to Woe.
On Conrad's stricken soul exhaustion prest,
And stupor almost lull'd it into rest;
So feeble now—his mother's softness crept
To those wild eyes, which like an infant's wept:
It was the very weakness of his brain,
Which thus confess'd without relieving pain.
None saw his trickling tears—perchance, if seen,   30
That useless flood of grief had never been:
Nor long they flow'd—he dried them to depart,
In helpless—hopeless—brokenness of heart:
The sun goes forth, but Conrad's day is dim;
And the night cometh—ne'er to pass from him.
There is no darkness like the cloud of mind,
On Grief's vain eye—the blindest of the blind!
Which may not—dare not see—but turns aside
To blackest shade—nor will endure a guide!

His heart was form'd for softness—warp'd to wrong;   40
Betray'd too early, and beguiled too long;
Each feeling pure—as falls the dropping dew
Within the grot—like that had harden'd too;
Less clear, perchance, its earthly trials pass'd,
But sunk, and chill'd, and petrified at last.
Yet tempests wear, and lightning cleaves the rock;
If such his heart, so shatter'd it the shock.
There grew one flower beneath its rugged brow,
Though dark the shade—it shelter'd—saved till now.
The thunder came—that bolt hath blasted both,   50
The Granite's firmness, and the Lily's growth:
The gentle plant hath left no leaf to tell
Its tale, but shrunk and wither'd where it fell;
And of its cold protector, blacken round
But shiver'd fragments on the barren ground!

And Thou art Dead, as Young and Fair

'*Heu, quanto minus est cum reliquis versari quam tui meminisse!*'

And thou art dead, as young and fair
    As aught of mortal birth;
And form so soft, and charms so rare,
    Too soon return'd to Earth!
Though Earth received them in her bed
And o'er the spot the crowd may tread
    In carelessness or mirth,
There is an eye which could not brook
A moment on that grave to look.

I will not ask where thou liest low,

Nor gaze upon the spot;
There flowers or weeds at will may grow,
So I behold them not:
It is enough for me to prove
That what I loved, and long must love,
Like common earth can rot;
To me there needs no stone to tell,
'Tis Nothing that I loved so well.

Yet did I love thee to the last
As fervently as thou,
Who didst not change through all the past,
And canst not alter now.
The love where Death has set his seal,
Nor age can chill, nor rival steal,
Nor falsehood disavow:
And, what were worse, thou canst not see
Or wrong, or change, or fault in me.

The better days of life were ours;
The worst can be but mine:
The sun that cheers, the storm that lowers
Shall never more be thine.
The silence of that dreamless sleep
I envy now too much to weep;
Nor need I to repine,
That all those charms have pass'd away:
I might have watch'd through long decay.

The flower in ripen'd bloom unmatch'd
Must fall the earliest prey;
Though by no hand untimely snatch'd,
The leaves must drop away:

35

And yet it were a greater grief
To watch it withering, leaf by leaf,
    Than see it pluck'd to-day;
Since earthly eye but ill can bear
To trace the change to foul from fair.

I know not if I could have borne
    To see thy beauties fade;
The night that follow'd such a morn
    Had worn a deeper shade:
Thy day without a cloud hath pass'd,   50
And thou wert lovely to the last;
    Extinguish'd, not decay'd;
As stars that shoot along the sky
Shine brightest as they fall from high.

As once I wept, if I could weep,
    My tears might well be shed,
To think I was not near to keep
    One vigil o'er thy bed;
To gaze, how fondly! on thy face,
To fold thee in a faint embrace,   60
    Uphold thy drooping head;
And show that love, however vain,
Nor thou nor I can feel again.

Yet how much less it were to gain,
    Though thou hast left me free,
The loveliest things that still remain,
    Than thus remember thee!
The all of thine that cannot die
Through dark and dread Eternity
    Returns again to me,   70
And more thy buried love endears
Than aught except its living years.

If Sometimes in the Haunts of Men

If sometimes in the haunts of men
   Thine image from my breast may fade,
The lonely hour presents again
   The semblance of thy gentle shade:
And now that sad and silent hour
   Thus much of thee can still restore,
And sorrow unobserved may pour
   The plaint she dare not speak before.

Oh, pardon that in crowds awhile
   I waste one thought I owe to thee,   10
And self-condemn'd, appear to smile,
   Unfaithful to thy memory:
Nor deem that memory less dear,
   That then I seem not to repine;
I would not fools should overhear
   One sigh that should be wholly *thine*.

If not the goblet pass unquaff'd,
   It is not drain'd to banish care;
The cup must hold a deadlier draught,
   That brings a Lethe for despair.   20
And could Oblivion set my soul
   From all her troubled visions free,
I'd dash to earth the sweetest bowl
   That drown'd a single thought of thee.

For wert thou vanish'd from my mind,
   Where could my vacant bosom turn?

And who would then remain behind
    To honour thine abandon'd Urn?
No, no—it is my sorrow's pride
    That last dear duty to fulfil;   30
Though all the world forget beside,
    'Tis meet that I remember still.

For well I know, that such had been
    Thy gentle care for him, who now
Unmourn'd shall quit this mortal scene,
    Where none regarded him, but thou:
And, oh! I feel in *that* was given
    A blessing never meant for me;
Thou wert too like a dream of Heaven
    For earthly Love to merit thee.   40

From

The Island

I

The fight was o'er; the flashing through the gloom,
Which robes the cannon as he wings a tomb,
Had ceased; and sulphury vapours upward driven
Had left the earth, and but polluted heaven:
The rattling roar which rung in every volley
Had left the echoes to their melancholy;
No more they shriek'd their horror, boom for boom;
The strife was done, the vanquish'd had their doom;
The mutineers were crush'd, dispers'd, or ta'en,
Or lived to deem the happiest were the slain,   10
Few, few escaped, and these were hunted o'er
The isle they loved beyond their native shore.

No further home was theirs, it seem'd, on earth,
Once renegades to that which gave them birth;
Track'd like wild beasts, like them they sought the wild,
As to a mother's bosom flies the child:
But vainly wolves and lions seek their den,
And still more vainly men escape from men.

II

Beneath a rock whose jutting base protrudes
Far over ocean in its fiercest moods,   20
When scaling his enormous crag the wave
Is hurl'd down headlong like the foremost brave,
And falls back on the foaming crowd behind,
Which fight beneath the banners of the wind,
But now at rest, a little remnant drew
Together, bleeding, thirsty, faint, and few;
But still their weapons in their hands, and still
With something of the pride of former will,
As men not all unused to meditate,
And strive much more than wonder at their fate.   30
Their present lot was what they had foreseen,
And dared as what was likely to have been;
Yet still the lingering hope, which deem'd their lot
Not pardon'd, but unsought for or forgot,
Or trusted that, if sought, their distant caves
Might still be miss'd amidst the world of waves,
Had wean'd their thoughts in part from what they saw
And felt, the vengeance of their country's law.
Their sea-green isle, their guilt-won paradise,
No more could shield their virtue or their vice: 40
Their better feelings, if such were, were thrown
Back on themselves,—their sins remain'd alone.
Proscribed even in their second country, they
Were lost; in vain the world before them lay;
All outlets seem'd secured. Their new allies

39

Had fought and bled in mutual sacrifice;
But what avail'd the club and spear, and arm
Of Hercules, against the sulphury charm,
The magic of the thunder, which destroy'd
The warrior ere his strength could be employ'd?   50
Dug, like a spreading pestilence, the grave
No less of human bravery than the brave!
Their own scant numbers acted all the few
Against the many oft will dare and do;
But though the choice seems native to die free,
Even Greece can boast but one Thermopylæ,
Till *now*, when she has forged her broken chain
Back to a sword, and dies and lives again!

III
Beside the jutting rock the few appear'd,
Like the last remnant of the red-deer's herd;   60
Their eyes were feverish, and their aspect worn,
But still the hunter's blood was on their horn,
A little stream came tumbling from the height,
And straggling into ocean as it might,
Its bounding crystal frolick'd in the ray,
And gush'd from cliff to crag with saltless spray;
Close on the wild, wide ocean, yet as pure
And fresh as innocence, and more secure,
Its silver torrent glitter'd o'er the deep,
As the shy chamois' eye o'erlooks the steep,   70
While far below the vast and sullen swell
Of ocean's alpine azure rose and fell.
To this young spring they rush'd,—all feelings first
Absorb'd in passion's and in nature's thrist,—
Drank as they do who drink their last, and threw
Their arms aside to revel in its dew;
Cool'd their scorch'd throats, and wash'd the gory stains
From wounds whose only bandage might be chains;

Then, when their drought was quench'd, look'd sadly round,
As wondering how so many still were found   80
Alive and fetterless:—but silent all,
Each sought his fellow's eyes, as if to call
On him for language which his lips denied,
As though their voices with their cause had died.

A Spirit Pass'd Before Me

FROM JOB

I

A spirit pass'd before me: I beheld
The face of immortality unveil'd—
Deep sleep came down on every eye save mine—
And there it stood,—all formless—but divine:
Along my bones the creeping flesh did quake;
And as my damp hair stiffen'd, thus it spake:

II

'Is man more just than God? Is man more pure
Than he who deems even Seraphs insecure?
Creatures of clay—vain dwellers in the dust!
The moth survives you, and are ye more just?   10
Things of a day! you wither ere the night,
Heedless and blind to Wisdom's wasted light!'

Lines on Hearing that Lady Byron was Ill

And thou wert sad—yet I was not with thee;
   And thou wert sick, and yet I was not near;

Methought that joy and health alone could be
    Where I was *not*—and pain and sorrow here!
And is it thus?—it is as I foretold,
    And shall be more so; for the mind recoils
Upon itself, and the wreck'd heart lies cold,
    While heaviness collects the shatter'd spoils.
It is not in the storm nor in the strife
    We feel benumb'd, and wish to be no more   10
    But in the after-silence on the shore,
When all is lost, except a little life.
I am too well avenged!—but 'twas my right;
    Whate'er my sins might be, *thou* wert not sent
To be the Nemesis who should requite—
    Nor did Heaven choose so near an instrument.
Mercy is for the merciful!—if thou
Hast been of such, 'twill be accorded now.
Thy nights are banish'd from the realms of sleep!—
    Yes! they may flatter thee, but thou shalt feel   20
    A hollow agony which will not heal,
For thou art pillow'd on a curse too deep;
Thou hast sown in my sorrow, and must reap
    The bitter harvest in a woe as real!
I have had many foes, but none like thee;
    For 'gainst the rest myself I could defend,
    And be avenged, or turn them into friend;
But thou in safe implacability
Hadst nought to dread—in thy own weakness shielded,
And in my love, which hath but too much yielded,   30
    And spared, for thy sake, some I should not spare;
And thus upon the world—trust in thy truth,
And the wild fame of my ungovern'd youth—
    On things that were not, and on things that are—
Even upon such a basis hast thou built
A monument, whose cement hath been guilt!
    The moral Clytemnestra of thy lord,

And hew'd down, with an unsuspected sword,
Fame, peace, and hope—and all the better life,
 Which, but for this cold treason of thy heart, 40
Might still have risen from out the grave of strife,
 And found a nobler duty than to part.
But of thy virtues didst thou make a vice.
 Trafficking with them in a purpose cold,
 For present anger, and for future gold—
And buying other's grief at any price.
And thus once enter'd into crooked ways,
The earthly truth, which was thy proper praise,
Did not still walk beside thee—but at times,
And with a breast unknowing its own crimes, 50
Deceit, averments incompatible,
Equivocations, and the thoughts which dwell
 In Janus-spirits—the significant eye
Which learns to lie with silence—the pretext
Of prudence, with advantages annex'd—
The acquiescence in all things which tend,
No matter how, to the desired end—
 All found a place in thy philosophy.
The means were worthy, and the end is won—
I would not do by thee as thou hast done! 60

Stanzas to Augusta

I

When all around grew drear and dark,
 And reason half withheld her ray—
And hope but shed a dying spark
 Which more misled my lonely way;

43

II

In that deep midnight of the mind,
  And that internal strife of heart,
When dreading to be deem'd too kind,
  The weak despair—the cold depart;

III

When fortune changed—and love fled far,
  And hatred's shafts flew thick and fast,   10
Thou wert the solitary star
  Which rose and set not to the last.

IV

Oh! blest be thine unbroken light!
  That watch'd me as a seraph's eye,
And stood between me and the night,
  For ever shining sweetly nigh.

V

And when the cloud upon us came,
  Which strove to blacken o'er thy ray—
Then purer spread its gentle flame,
  And dash'd the darkness all away.   20

VI

Still may thy spirit dwell on mine,
  And teach it what to brave or brook—
There's more in one soft word of thine
  Than in the world's defied rebuke.

VII

Thou stood'st, as stands a lovely tree,
  That still unbroke, though gently bent,
Still waves with fond fidelity
  Its boughs above a monument.

44

VIII

The winds might rend—the skies might pour,
    But there thou wert—and still wouldst be   30
Devoted in the stormiest hour
    To shed thy weeping leaves o'er me.

IX

But thou and thine shall know no blight,
    Whatever fate on me may fall;
For heaven in sunshine will requite
    The kind—and thee the most of all.

X

Then let the ties of baffled love
    Be broken—thine will never break;
Thy heart can feel—but will not move;
    Thy soul, though soft, will never shake.   40

XI

And these, when all was lost beside,
    Were found and still are fix'd in thee;—
And bearing still a breast so tried,
    Earth is no desert—ev'n to me.

On This Day I complete my Thirty-Sixth Year

'Tis time this heart should be unmoved,
    Since others it hath ceased to move:
Yet, though I cannot be beloved,
    Still let me love!

45

My days are in the yellow leaf;
   The flowers and fruits of love are gone;
The worm, the canker, and the grief
     Are mine alone!

The fire that on my bosom preys
   Is lone as some volcanic isle;
No torch is kindled at its blaze—
     A funeral pile.

The hope, the fear, the jealous care,
   The exalted portion of the pain
And power of love, I cannot share,
     But wear the chain.

But 'tis not *thus*—and 'tis not *here*—
   Such thoughts should shake my soul, nor *now*,
Where glory decks the hero's bier,
     Or binds his brow.

The sword, the banner, and the field,
   Glory and Greece, around me see!
The Spartan, borne upon his shield,
     Was not more free.

Awake! (not Greece—she *is* awake!)
   Awake, my spirit! Think through *whom*
Thy life-blood tracks its parent lake,
     And then strike home!

Tread those reviving passions down,
   Unworthy manhood!—unto thee
Indifferent should the smile or frown
     Of beauty be.

If thou regrett'st thy youth, *why live?*
    The land of honourable death
Is here:—up to the field, and give
    Away thy breath!

Seek out—less often sought than found—
    A soldier's grave, for thee the best;
Then look around, and choose thy ground,
    And take thy rest.   40

MISSOLONGHI, Jan. 22, 1824

To Time

Time! on whose arbitrary wing
    The varying hours must flag or fly,
Whose tardy winter, fleeting spring,
    But drag or drive us on to die—

Hail thou! who on my birth bestow'd
    Those boons to all that know thee known;
Yet better I sustain thy load,
    For now I bear the weight alone.

I would not one fond heart should share
    The bitter moments thou hast given;   10
And pardon thee, since thou could'st spare
    All that I loved, to peace or heaven.

To them be joy or rest, on me
    Thy future ills shall press in vain;
I nothing owe but years to thee,
    A debt already paid in pain.

Yet even that pain was some relief,
   It felt, but still forgot thy power:
The active agony of grief
   Retards, but never counts the hour.   20

In joy I've sigh'd to think thy flight
   Would soon subside from swift to slow;
Thy cloud could overcast the light,
   But could not add a night to woe;

For then, however, drear and dark,
   My soul was suited to thy sky;
One star alone shot forth a spark
   To prove thee—not Eternity.

That beam hath sunk, and now thou art
   A blank; a thing to count and curse,   30
Through each dull tedious trifling part,
   Which all regret, yet all rehearse.

One scene even thou canst not deform;
   The limit of thy sloth or speed
When future wanderers bear the storm
   Which we shall sleep too sound to heed:

And I can smile to think how weak
   Thine efforts shortly shall be shown,
When all the vengeance thou canst wreak
   Must fall upon—a nameless stone.   40

PART TWO

LONGER POEMS AND EXTRACTS

From

Childe Harold's Pilgrimage

Canto Four

XCIII

What from this barren being do we reap?
Our senses narrow, and our reason frail,
Life short, and truth a gem which loves the deep,
And all things weigh'd in custom's falsest scale;
Opinion an omnipotence,—whose veil
Mantles the earth with darkness, until right
And wrong are accidents, and men grow pale
Lest their own judgments should become too bright,
And their free thoughts be crimes, and earth have too much light.

XCIV

And thus they plod in sluggish misery,   10
Rotting from sire to son, and age to age,
Proud of their trampled nature, and so die,
Bequeathing their hereditary rage
To the new race of inborn slaves, who wage
War for their chains, and rather than be free,
Bleed gladiator-like, and still engage
Within the same arena where they see
Their fellows fall before, like leaves of the same tree.

I speak not of men's creeds—they rest between
Man and his Maker—but of things allow'd,   20
Averr'd, and known, and daily, hourly seen—
The yoke that is upon us doubly bow'd,
And the intent of tyranny avow'd.
The edict of Earth's rulers, who are grown
The apes of him who humbled once the proud,
And shook them from their slumbers on the throne:
Too glorious, were this all his mighty arm had done.

Can tyrants but by tyrants conquer'd be,
And Freedom find no champion and no child
Such as Columbia saw arise when she   30
Sprung forth a Pallas, arm'd and undefiled?
Or must such minds be nourish'd in the wild,
Deep in the unpruned forest, 'midst the roar
Of cataracts, where nursing Nature smiled
On infant Washington? Has Earth no more
Such seeds within her breast, or Europe no such shore?

But France got drunk with blood to vomit crime,
And fatal have her Saturnalia been
To Freedom's cause, in every age and clime;
Because the deadly days which we have seen,   40
And vile Ambition, that built up between
Man and his hopes an adamantine wall,
And the base pageant last upon the scene,
Are grown the pretext for the eternal thrall
Which nips life's tree, and dooms man's worst—his second fall.

Yet, Freedom! yet thy banner, torn, but flying,
Streams like the thunder-storm *against* the wind;

Thy trumpet voice, though broken now and dying,
The loudest still the tempest leaves behind;
Thy tree hath lost its blossoms, and the rind,   50
Chopp'd by the axe, looks rough and little worth,
But the sap lasts,—and still the seed we find
Sown deep, even in the bosom of the North;
So shall a better spring less bitter fruit bring forth.

* * * * *

CXXII

Of its own beauty is the mind diseased,
And fevers into false creation:—where,
Where are the forms the sculptor's soul hath seiz'd?
In him alone. Can Nature show so fair?
Where are the charms and virtues which we dare
Conceive in boyhood and pursue as men,   60
The unreach'd Paradise of our despair,
Which o'er-informs the pencil and the pen,
And overpowers the page where it would bloom again?

CXXIII

Who loves, raves—'tis youth's frenzy—but the cure
Is bitterer still, as charm by charm unwinds
Which robed our idols, and we see too sure
Nor worth nor beauty dwells from out the mind's
Ideal shape of such; yet still it binds
The fatal spell, and still it draws us on,
Reaping the whirlwind from the oft-sown winds;   70
The stubborn heart, its alchemy begun,
Seems ever near the prize—wealthiest when most undone.

CXXIV

We wither from our youth, we gasp away—
Sick—sick; unfound the boon, unslaked the thirst,

Though to the last, in verge of our decay,
Some phantom lures, such as we sought at first—
But all too late,—so are we doubly curst.
Love, fame, ambition, avarice—'tis the same,
Each idle, and all ill, and none the worst—
For all are meteors with a different name,   80
And Death the sable smoke where vanishes the flame.

CXXV

Few—none—find what they love or could have loved,
Though accident, blind contact, and the strong
Necessity of loving, have removed
Antipathies—but to recur, ere long,
Envenom'd with irrevocable wrong;
And Circumstance, that unspiritual god
And miscreator, makes and helps along
Our coming evils with a crutch-like rod,
Whose touch turns Hope to dust,—the dust we all have trod.   90

CXXVI

Our life is a false nature: 'tis not in
The harmony of things,—this hard decree,
This uneradicable taint of sin,
This boundless upas, this all-blasting tree,
Whose root is earth, whose leaves and branches be
The skies which rain their plagues on men like dew—
Disease, death, bondage—all the woes we see,
And worse, the woes we see not—which throb through
The immedicable soul, with heart-aches ever new.

CXXVII

Yet let us ponder boldly—'tis a base   100
Abandonment of reason to resign
Our right of thought—our last and only place

Of refuge; this, at least, shall still be mine:
Though from our birth the faculty divine
Is chain'd and tortured—cabin'd, cribb'd, confined,
And bred in darkness, lest the truth should shine
Too brightly on the unprepared mind,
The beam pours in, for time and skill will couch the blind.

CXXVIII

Arches on arches! as it were that Rome,
Collecting the chief trophies of her line,   110
Would build up all her triumphs in one dome,
Her Coliseum stands; the moonbeams shine
As 'twere its natural torches, for divine
Should be the light which streams here to illume
This long-explored but still exhaustless mine
Of contemplation; and the azure gloom
Of an Italian night, where the deep skies assume

CXXIX

Hues which have words, and speak to ye of heaven,
Floats o'er this vast and wondrous monument,
And shadows forth its glory. There is given   120
Unto the things of earth, which Time hath bent,
A spirit's feeling, and where he hath leant
His hand, but broke his scythe, there is a power
And magic in the ruin'd battlement,
For which the palace of the present hour
Must yield its pomp, and wait till ages are it's dower.

CXXX

Oh Time! the beautifier of the dead,
Adorner of the ruin, comforter
And only healer when the heart hath bled;
Time! the corrector where our judgments err,   130

53

The test of truth, love—sole philosopher,
For all beside are sophists—from thy thrift,
Which never loses though it doth defer—
Time, the avenger! unto thee I lift
My hands, and eyes, and heart, and crave of thee a gift:

CXXXI

Amidst this wreck, where thou hast made a shrine
And temple more divinely desolate,
Among thy mightier offerings here are mine,
Ruins of years, though few, yet full of fate:
If thou hast ever seen me too elate,   140
Hear me not; but if calmly I have borne
Good, and reserved my pride against the hate
Which shall not whelm me, let me not have worn
This iron in my soul in vain—shall *they* not mourn?

CXXXII

And thou, who never yet of human wrong
Left the unbalanced scale, great Nemesis!
Here, where the ancient paid thee homage long—
Thou who didst call the Furies from the abyss,
And round Orestes bade them howl and hiss
For that unnatural retribution—just,   150
Had it but been from hands less near—in this
Thy former realm, I call thee from the dust!
Dost thou not hear my heart?—Awake! thou shalt, and must.

CXXXIII

It is not that I may not have incurr'd
For my ancestral faults or mine the wound
I bleed withal, and, had it been conferr'd
With a just weapon, it had flow'd unbound;

But now my blood shall not sink in the ground;
To thee I do devote it—*thou* shalt take
The vengeance, which shall yet be sought and found,   160
Which if *I* have not taken for the sake—
But let that pass—I sleep, but thou shalt yet awake.

CXXXIV

And if my voice break forth, 'tis not that now
I shrink from what is suffer'd: let him speak
Who hath beheld decline upon my brow,
Or seen my mind's convulsion leave it weak;
But in this page a record will I seek.
Not in the air shall these my words disperse,
Though I be ashes; a far hour shall wreak
The deep prophetic fulness of this verse,   170
And pile on human heads the mountain of my curse!

CXXXV

That curse shall be Forgiveness.—Have I not—
Hear me, my mother Earth! behold it, Heaven!
Have I not had to wrestle with my lot?
Have I not suffer'd things to be forgiven?
Have I not had my brain sear'd, my heart riven,
Hopes sapp'd, name blighted, Life's life lied away?
And only not to desperation driven,
Because not altogether of such clay
As rots into the souls of those whom I survey.   180

★   ★   ★   ★   ★

CLXXVII

Oh! that the Desert were my dwelling-place,
With one fair Spirit for my minister,
That I might all forget the human race,
And, hating no one, love but only her!

Ye elements!—in whose ennobling stir
I feel myself exalted—Can ye not
Accord me such a being? Do I err
In deeming such inhabit many a spot?
Though with them to converse can rarely be our lot.

CLXXVIII

There is a pleasure in the pathless woods,   190
There is a rapture on the lonely shore,
There is society, where none intrudes,
By the deep Sea, and music in its roar:
I love not Man the less, but Nature more,
From these our interviews, in which I steal
From all I may be, or have been before,
To mingle with the Universe, and feel
What I can ne'er express, yet cannot all conceal.

CLXXIX

Roll on, thou deep and dark blue Ocean—roll!
Ten thousand fleets sweep over thee in vain;   200
Man marks the earth with ruin—his control
Stops with the shore; upon the watery plain
The wrecks are all thy deed, nor doth remain
A shadow of man's ravage, save his own,
When, for a moment, like a drop of rain,
He sinks into thy depths with bubbling groan,
Without a grave, unknell'd, uncoffin'd, and unknown.

CLXXX

His steps are not upon thy paths,—thy fields
Are not a spoil for him,—thou dost arise
And shake him from thee; the vile strength he wields   210
For earth's destruction thou dost all depise,
Spurning him from thy bosom to the skies,

And send'st him, shivering in thy playful spray
And howling, to his Gods, where haply lies
His petty hope in some near port or bay,
And dashest him again to earth:—there let him lay

CLXXXI

The armaments which thunderstrike the walls
Of rock-built cities, bidding nations quake,
And monarchs tremble in their capitals,
The oak leviathans, whose huge ribs make   220
Their clay creator the vain title take
Of lord of thee, and arbiter of war—
These are thy toys, and, as the snowy flake,
They melt into the yeast of waves, which mar
Alike the Armada's pride or spoils of Trafalgar.

CLXXXII

Thy shores are empires, changed in all save thee—
Assyria, Greece, Rome, Carthage, what are they?
Thy waters wash'd them power while they were free,
And many a tyrant since; their shores obey
The stranger, slave, or savage; their decay   230
Has dried up realms to deserts:—not so thou;—
Unchangeable, save to thy wild waves' play,
Time writes no wrinkle on thine azure brow:
Such as creation's dawn beheld, thou rollest now.

CLXXXIII

Thou glorious mirror, where the Almighty's form
Glasses itself in tempests; in all time,—
Calm or convulsed, in breeze, or gale, or storm,
Icing the pole, or in the torrid clime
Dark-heaving—boundless, endless, and sublime,
The image of eternity, the throne   240
Of the Invisible; even from out thy slime

57

The monsters of the deep are made; each zone
Obeys thee; thou goest forth, dread, fathomless, alone.

CLXXXIV

And I have loved thee, Ocean! and my joy
Of youthful sports was on thy breast to be
Borne, like thy bubbles, onward: from a boy
I wanton'd with thy breakers—they to me
Were a delight; and if the freshening sea
Made them a terror—'twas a pleasing fear,
For I was as it were a child of thee,   250
And trusted to thy billows far and near,
And laid my hand upon thy mane—as I do here.

CLXXXV

My task is done, my song hath ceased, my theme
Has died into an echo; it is fit
The spell should break of this protracted dream.
The torch shall be extinguish'd which hath lit
My midnight lamp—and what is writ, is writ;
Would it were worthier! but I am not now
That which I have been—and my visions flit
Less palpably before me—and the glow   260
Which in my spirit dwelt is fluttering, faint, and low.

CLXXXVI

Farewell! a word that must be, and hath been—
A sound which makes us linger;—yet—farewell!
Ye! who have traced the Pilgrim to the scene
Which is his last, if in your memories dwell
A thought which once was his, if on ye swell
A single recollection, not in vain
He wore his sandal-shoon and scallop-shell;
Farewell! with *him* alone may rest the pain,
If such there were—with *you*, the moral of his strain   270

The Siege of Corinth

In the year since Jesus died for men,
Eighteen hundred years and ten,
We were a gallant company,
Riding o'er land, and sailing o'er sea.
Oh! but we went merrily!
We forded the river, and clomb the high hill,
Never our steeds for a day stood still;
Whether we lay in the cave or the shed,
Our sleep fell soft on the hardest bed:
Whether we couch'd in our rough capote,   10
On the rougher plank of our gliding boat,
Or stretch'd on the beach, or our saddles spread
As a pillow beneath the resting head,
Fresh we woke upon the morrow:
   All our thoughts and words had scope,
   We had health, and we had hope,
Toil and travel, but no sorrow.
We were of all tongues and creeds:—
Some were those who counted beads,
Some of mosque, and some of church,   20
   And some, or I mis-say, of neither;
Yet through the wide world might ye search,
   Nor find a motlier crew nor blither.
But some are dead, and some are gone,
And some are scatter'd and alone,
And some are rebels on the hills
   That look along Epirus' valleys,
   Where freedom still at moments rallies,
And pays in blood oppression's ills;
   And some are in a far countree,   30

And some all restlessly at home;
  But never more, oh! never, we
Shall meet to revel and to roam.

But those hardy days flew cheerily!
And when they now fall drearily,
My thoughts, like swallows, skim the main,
And bear my spirit back again
Over the earth, and through the air,
A wild bird and a wanderer.
'Tis this that ever wakes my strain,   40
And oft, too oft, implores again
The few who may endure my lay,
To follow me so far away.
Stranger—wilt thou follow now,
And sit with me on Acro-Corinth's brow?

I

Many a vanish'd year and age,
And tempest's breath, and battle's rage,
Have swept o'er Corinth; yet she stands,
A fortress form'd to Freedom's hands.
The whirlwind's wrath, the earthquake's shock,   50
Have left untouch'd her hoary rock,
The keystone of a land, which still,
Though fall'n, looks proudly on that hill,
The landmark to the double tide
That purpling rolls on either side,
As if their waters chafed to meet,
Yet pause and crouch beneath her feet.
But could the blood before her shed
Since first Timoleon's brother bled,
Or baffled Persia's despot fled,   60
Arise from out the earth which drank
The stream of slaughter as it sank,

That sanguine ocean would o'erflow
Her isthmus idly spread below:
Or could the bones of all the slain,
Who perish'd there, be piled again,
That rival pyramid would rise
More mountain-like, through those clear skies,
Than yon tower-capp'd Acropolis,
Which seems the very clouds to kiss.   70

II

On dun Cithæron's ridge appears
The gleam of twice ten thousand spears;
And downward to the Isthmian plain,
From shore to shore of either main,
The tent is pitch'd, the crescent shines
Along the Moslem's leaguering lines;
And the dusk Spahi's bands advance
Beneath each bearded pacha's glance;
And far and wide as eye can reach
The turban'd cohorts throng the beach;   80
And there the Arab's camel kneels,
And there his steed the Tartar wheels;
The Turcoman hath left his herd,
The sabre round his loins to gird;
And there the volleying thunders pour,
Till waves grow smoother to the roar.
The trench is dug, the cannon's breath
Wings the far hissing globe of death;
Fast whirl the fragments from the wall,
Which crumbles with the ponderous ball;   90
And from that wall the foe replies,
O'er dusty plain and smoky skies,
With fires that answer fast and well
The summons of the Infidel.

61

III

But near and nearest to the wall
Of those who wish and work its fall,
With deeper skill in war's black art
Than Othman's sons, and high of heart
As any chief that ever stood
Triumphant in the fields of blood;   100
From post to post, and deed to deed,
Fast spurring on his reeking steed,
Where sallying ranks the trench assail,
And make the foremost Moslem quail;
Or where the battery, guarded well,
Remains as yet impregnable,
Alighting cheerly to inspire
The soldier slackening in his fire;
The first and freshest of the host
Which Stamboul's sultan there can boast,   110
To guide the follower o'er the field,
To point the tube, the lance to wield,
Or whirl around the bickering blade;—
Was Alp, the Adrian renegade!

IV

From Venice—once a race of worth
His gentle sires—he drew his birth;
But late an exile from her shore,
Against his countrymen he bore
The arms they taught to bear; and now
The turban girt his shaven brow.   120
Through many a change had Corinth pass'd
With Greece to Venice' rule at last;
And here, before her walls, with those
To Greece and Venice equal foes,
He stood a foe, with all the zeal
Which young and fiery converts feel,

Within whose heated bosom throngs
The memory of a thousand wrongs.
To him had Venice ceased to be
Her ancient civic boast—'the Free';   130
And in the palace of St. Mark
Unnamed accusers in the dark
Within the 'Lion's mouth' had placed
A charge against him uneffaced:
He fled in time, and saved his life,
To waste his future years in strife,
That taught his land how great her loss
In him who triumph'd o'er the Cross,
'Gainst which he rear'd the Crescent high,
And battled to avenge or die.   140

V

Coumourgi—he whose closing scene
Adorn'd the triumph of Eugene,
When on Carlowitz' bloody plain,
The last and mightiest of the slain,
He sank, regretting not to die,
But cursed the Christian's victory—
Coumourgi—can his glory cease,
That latest conqueror of Greece,
Till Christian hands to Greece restore
The freedom Venice gave of yore?   150
A hundred years have roll'd away
Since he refix'd the Moslem's sway;
And now he led the Mussulman,
And gave the guidance of the van
To Alp, who well repaid the trust
By cities levell'd with the dust;
And proved, by many a deed of death,
How firm his heart in novel faith.

The walls grew weak; and fast and hot
Against them pour'd the ceaseless shot,   160
With unabating fury sent
From battery to battlement;
And thunder-like the pealing din
Rose from each heated culverin;
And here and there some crackling dome
Was fired before the exploding bomb;
And as the fabric sank beneath
The shattering shell's volcanic breath,
In red and wreathing columns flash'd
The flame, as loud the ruin crash'd,   170
Or into countless meteors driven,
Its earth-stars melted into heaven;
Whose clouds that day grew doubly dun,
Impervious to the hidden sun,
With volumed smoke that slowly grew.
To one wide sky of sulphurous hue.

VII

But not for vengeance, long delay'd,
Alone, did Alp, the renegade,
The Moslem warriors sternly teach
His skill to pierce the promised breach: 180
Within these walls a maid was pent
His hope would win, without consent
Of that inexorable sire,
Whose heart refused him in its ire,
When Alp, beneath his Christian name,
Her virgin hand aspired to claim.
In happier mood, and earlier time,
While unimpeach'd for traitorous crime,
Gayest in gondola or hall,
He glitter'd through the Carnival;   190

And tuned the softest serenade
That e'er on Adria's waters play'd
At midnight to Italian maid.

VIII

And many deem'd her heart was won;
For sought by numbers, given to none,
Had young Francesca's hand remain'd
Still by the church's bonds unchain'd:
And when the Adriatic bore
Lanciotto to the Paynim shore,
Her wonted smiles were seen to fail,   200
And pensive wax'd the maid and pale;
More constant at confessional,
More rare at masque and festival;
Or seen at such, with downcast eyes,
Which conquer'd hearts they ceased to prize;
With listless look she seems to gaze:
With humbler care her form arrays;
Her voice less lively in the song;
Her step, though light, less fleet among
The pairs, on whom the Morning's glance   210
Breaks, yet unsated with the dance.

IX

Sent by the state to guard the land,
(Which, wrested from the Moslem's hand,
While Sobieski tamed his pride
By Buda's wall and Danube's side,
The chiefs of Venice wrung away
From Patra to Eubœa's bay,)
Minotti held in Corinth's towers
The Doge's delegated powers,
While yet the pitying eye of Peace   220
Smiled o'er her long forgotten Greece:

65

And ere that faithless truce was broke
Which freed her from the unchristian yoke,
With him his gentle daughter came;
Nor there, since Menelaus' dame
Forsook her lord and land, to prove
What woes await on lawless love,
Had fairer form adorn'd the shore
Than she, the matchless stranger, bore.

x

The wall is rent, the ruins yawn;   230
And with to-morrow's earliest dawn,
O'er the disjointed mass shall vault
The foremost of the fierce assault.
The bands are rank'd; the chosen van
Of Tartar and of Mussulman,
The full of hope, misnamed 'forlorn',
Who hold the thought of death in scorn,
And win their way with falchion's force,
Or pave the path with many a corse,
O'er which the following brave may rise,   240
Their stepping-stone—the last who dies!

xi

'Tis midnight: on the mountains brown
The cold, round moon shines deeply down;
Blue roll the waters, blue the sky
Spreads like an ocean hung on high,
Bespangled with those isles of light,
So wildly, spiritually bright,
Who ever gazed upon them shining
And turn'd to earth without repining,
Nor wish'd for wings to flee away,   250
And mix with their eternal ray?
The waves on either shore lay there

66

Calm, clear, and azure as the air;
And scarce their foam the pebbles shook,
But murmur'd meekly as the brook.
The winds were pillow'd on the waves;
The banners droop'd along their staves,
And, as they fell around them furling,
Above them shone the crescent curling;
And that deep silence was unbroke,   260
Save where the watch his signal spoke,
Save where the steed neigh'd oft and shrill,
And echo answer'd from the hill,
And the wide hum of that wild host
Rustled like leaves from coast to coast,
As rose the Muezzin's voice in air
In midnight call to wonted prayer;
It rose, that chanted mournful strain,
Like some lone spirit's o'er the plain:
'Twas musical, but sadly sweet,   270
Such as when winds and harp-strings meet,
And take a long unmeasured tone,
To mortal minstrelsy unknown.
It seem'd to those within the wall
A cry prophetic of their fall:
It struck even the besieger's ear
With something ominous and drear,
An undefined and sudden thrill,
Which makes the heart a moment still,
Then beat with quicker pulse, ashamed   280
Of that strange sense its silence framed;
Such as a sudden passing-bell
Wakes, though but for a stranger's knell.

XII
The tent of Alp was on the shore;
The sound was hush'd, the prayer was o'er,

The watch was set, the night-round made,
All mandates issued and obey'd:
'Tis but another anxious night,
His pains the morrow may requite
With all revenge and love can pay,   290
In guerdon for their long delay.
Few hours remain, and he hath need
Of rest, to nerve for many a deed
Of slaughter; but within his soul
The thoughts like troubled waters roll.
He stood alone among the host;
Not his the loud fanatic boast
To plant the crescent o'er the cross,
Or risk a life with little loss,
Secure in paradise to be   300
By Houris loved immortally:
Nor his, what burning patriots feel,
The stern exaltedness of zeal,
Profuse of blood, untired in toil,
When battling on the parent soil.
He stood alone—a renegade
Against the country he betray'd;
He stood alone amidst his band,
Without a trusted heart or hand:
They follow'd him, for he was brave,   310
And great the spoil he got and gave;
They crouch'd to him, for he had skill
To warp and wield the vulgar will:
But still his Christian origin
With them was little less than sin.
They envied even the faithless fame
He earn'd beneath a Moslem name;
Since he, their mightiest chief, had been
In youth a bitter Nazarene.
They did not know how pride can stoop,   320

When baffled feelings withering droop;
They did not know how hate can burn
In hearts once changed from soft to stern;
Nor all the false and fatal zeal
The convert of revenge can feel.
He ruled them—man may rule the worst,
By ever daring to be first:
So lions o'er the jackal sway;
The jackal points, he fells the prey,
Then on the vulgar, yelling, press,   330
To gorge the relics of success.

XIII
His head grows fever'd, and his pulse
The quick successive throbs convulse:
In vain from side to side he throws
His form, in courtship of repose;
Or if he dozed, a sound, a start
Awoke him with a sunken heart.
The turban on his hot bow press'd,
The mail weigh'd lead-like on his breast,
Though oft and long beneath its weight   340
Upon his eyes had slumber sate,
Without or couch or canopy,
Except a rougher field and sky
Than now might yield a warrior's bed,
Than now along the heaven was spread.
He could not rest, he could not stay
Within his tent to wait for day,
But walk'd him forth along the sand,
Where thousand sleepers strew'd the strand
What pillow'd them? and why should he   350
More wakeful than the humblest be,
Since more their peril, worse their toil?
And yet they fearless dream of spoil;

While he alone, where thousands pass'd
A night of sleep, perchance their last,
In sickly vigil wander'd on,
And envied all he gazed upon.

XIV

He felt his soul become more light
Beneath the freshness of the night.
Cool was the silent sky, though calm,   360
And bathed his brow with airy balm:
Behind, the camp—before him lay,
In many a winding creek and bay,
Lepanto's gulf; and, on the brow
Of Delphi's hill, unshaken snow,
High and eternal, such as shone
Through thousand summers brightly gone,
Along the gulf, the mount, the clime;
It will not melt, like man, to time:
Tyrant and slave are swept away,   370
Less form'd to wear before the ray;
But that white veil, the lightest, frailest,
Which on the mighty mount thou hailest,
While tower and tree are torn and rent,
Shines o'er its craggy battlement;
In form a peak, in height a cloud,
In texture like a hovering shroud,
Thus high by parting Freedom spread,
As from her fond abode she fled,
And linger'd on the spot, where long   380
Her prophet spirit spake in song.
Oh! still her step at moments falters
O'er wither'd fields, and ruin'd altars,
And fain would wake, in souls too broken,
By pointing to each glorious token:
But vain her voice, till better days

Dawn in those yet remember'd rays,
Which shone upon the Persian flying,
And saw the Spartan smile in dying.

XV

Not mindless of these mighty times   390
Was Alp, despite his flight and crimes;
And through this night, as on he wander'd,
And o'er the past and present ponder'd,
And thought upon the glorious dead
Who there in better cause had bled,
He felt how faint and feebly dim
The fame that could accrue to him,
Who cheer'd the band, and waved the sword,
A traitor in a turban'd horde;
And led them to the lawless siege,   400
Whose best success were sacrilege.
Not so had those his fancy number'd,
The chiefs whose dust around him slumber'd;
Their phalanx marshall'd on the plain,
Whose bulwarks were not then in vain.
They fell devoted, but undying;
The very gale their name seem'd sighing;
The waters murmur'd of their name;
The woods were peopled with their fame;
The silent pillar, lone and grey,   410
Claim'd kindred with their sacred clay;
Their spirits wrapp'd the dusky mountain,
Their memory sparkled o'er the fountain:
The meanest rill, the mightiest river
Roll'd mingling with their fame for ever.
Despite of every yoke she bears,
That land is glory's still and theirs!
'Tis still a watchword to the earth:
When man would do a deed of worth

He points to Greece, and turns to tread,   420
So sanction'd, on the tyrant's head:
He looks to her, and rushes on
Where life is lost, or freedom won.

XVI

Still by the shore Alp mutely mused,
And woo'd the freshness Night diffused.
There shrinks no ebb in that tideless sea,
Which changeless rolls eternally;
So that wildest of waves, in their angriest mood,
Scarce break on the bounds of the land for a rood;
And the powerless moon beholds them flow,   430
Heedless if she come or go:
Calm or high, in main or bay,
On their course she hath no sway.
The rock unworn its base doth bare,
And looks o'er the surf, but it comes not there;
And the fringe of the foam may be seen below,
On the line that it left long ages ago:
A smooth short space of yellow sand
Between it and the greener land.

He wander'd on along the beach,   440
Till within the range of a carbine's reach
Of the leaguer'd wall; but they saw him not,
Or how could he 'scape from the hostile shot?
Did traitors lurk in the Christians' hold?
Were their hands grown stiff, or their hearts wax'd cold?
I know not, in sooth; but from yonder wall
There flash'd no fire, and there hiss'd no ball,
Though he stood beneath the bastion's frown,
That flank'd the sea-ward gate of the town;
Though he heard the sound, and could almost tell   450
The sullen words of the sentinel,

72

As his measured step on the stone below
Clank'd, as he paced it to and fro;
And he saw the lean dogs beneath the wall
Hold o'er the dead their carnival,
Gorging and growling o'er carcass and limb;
They were too busy to bark at him!
From a Tartar's skull they had stripp'd the flesh,
As ye peel the fig when its fruit is fresh;
And their white tusks crunch'd o'er the whiter skull,   460
As it slipp'd through their jaws, when their edge grew dull,
As they lazily mumbled the bones of the dead,
When they scarce could rise from the spot where they fed;
So well had they broken a lingering fast
With those who had fallen for that night's repast.
And Alp knew, by the turbans that roll'd on the sand,
The foremost of these were the best of his band:
Crimson and green were the shawls of their wear,
And each scalp had a single long tuft of hair,
All the rest was shaven and bare.   470
The scalps were in the wild dog's maw,
The hair was tangled round his jaw:
But close by the shore, on the edge of the gulf,
There sat a vulture flapping a wolf,
Who had stolen from the hills, but kept away,
Scared by the dogs, from the human prey;
But he seized on his share of a steed that lay,
Pick'd by the birds, on the sands of the bay.

                               XVII
Alp turn'd him from the sickening sight:
Never had shaken his nerves in fight;   480
But he better could brook to behold the dying,
Deep in the tide of their warm blood lying,
Scorch'd with the death-thirst, and writhing in vain,
Than the perishing dead who are past all pain.

                               73

There is something of pride in the perilous hour,
Whate'er be the shape in which death may lower;
For Fame is there to say who bleeds,
And Honour's eye on daring deeds!
But when all is past, it is humbling to tread
O'er the weltering field of the tombless dead,   490
And see worms of the earth, and fowls of the air,
Beasts of the forest, all gathering there;
All regarding man as their prey,
All rejoicing in his decay.

XVIII

There is a temple in ruin stands,
Fashion'd by long-forgotten hands;
Two or three columns, and many a stone,
Marble and granite, with grass o'ergrown!
Out upon Time! it will leave no more
Of the things to come than the things before!   500
Out upon Time! who for ever will leave
But enough of the past for the future to grieve
O'er that which hath been, and o'er that which must be:
What we have seen, our sons shall see;
Remnants of things that have pass'd away,
Fragments of stone rear'd by creatures of clay!

XIX

He sate him down at a pillar's base,
And pass'd his hand athwart his face;
Like one in dreary musing mood,
Declining was his attitude;   510
His head was drooping on his breast,
Fever'd, throbbing, and oppress'd;
And o'er his brow, so downward bent,
Oft his beating fingers went,
Hurriedly, as you may see

74

Your own run over the ivory key,
Ere the measured tone is taken
By the chords you would awaken.
There he sate all heavily,
As he heard the night-wind sigh.   520
Was it the wind through some hollow stone
Sent that soft and tender moan?
He lifted his head, and he look'd on the sea,
But it was unrippled as glass may be;
He look'd on the long grass—it waved not a blade;
How was that gentle sound convey'd?
He look'd to the banners—each flag lay still,
So did the leaves on Cithæron's hill,
And he felt not a breath come over his cheek;
What did that sudden sound bespeak?   530
He turn'd to the left—is he sure of sight?
There sate a lady, youthful and bright!

xx

He started up with more of fear
Than if an armed foe were near.
'God of my fathers! what is here?
Who art thou? and wherefore sent
So near a hostile armament?'
His trembling hands refused to sign
The cross he deem'd no more divine:
He had resumed it in that hour,   540
But conscience wrung away the power.
He gazed, he saw: he knew the face
Of beauty, and the form of grace;
It was Francesca by his side,
The maid who might have been his bride!

The rose was yet upon her cheek,
But mellow'd with a tenderer streak:

75

Where was the play of her soft lips fled?
Gone was the smile that enliven'd their red.
The ocean's calm within their view,   550
Beside her eye had less of blue;
But like that cold wave it stood still,
And its glance, though clear, was chill.
Around her form a thin robe twining,
Nought conceeal'd her bosom shining;
Through the parting of her hair,
Floating darkly downward there,
Her rounded arm show'd white and bare:
And ere yet she made reply,
Once she raised her hand on high;   560
It was so wan, and transparent of hue,
You might have seen the moon shine through.

XXI

'I come from my rest to him I love best,
That I may be happy, and he may be bless'd,
I have pass'd the guards, the gate, the wall;
Sought thee in safety through foes and all.
'Tis said the lion will turn and flee
From a maid in the pride of her purity;
And the Power on high, that can shield the good
Thus from the tyrant of the wood,   570
Hath extended its mercy to guard me as well
From the hands of the leaguering infidel.
I come—and if I come in vain,
Never, oh never, we meet again!
Thou hast done a fearful deed
In falling away from thy fathers' creed:
But dash that turban to earth, and sign
The sign of the cross, and for ever be mine;
Wring the black drop from thy heart,
And to-morrow unites us no more to part.'   580

76

'And where should our bridal couch be spread?
In the midst of the dying and the dead?
For to-morrow we give to the slaughter and flame
The sons and the shrines of the Christian name.
None, save thou and thine, I've sworn,
Shall be left upon the morn:
But thee will I bear to a lovely spot,
Where our hands shall be join'd, and our sorrow forgot.
There thou yet shalt be my bride,
When once again I've quell'd the pride   590
Of Venice; and her hated race
Have felt the arm they would debase
Scourge, with a whip of scorpions, those
Whom vice and envy made my foes.'

Upon his hand she laid her own—
Light was the touch, but it thrill'd to the bone,
And shot a chillness to his heart,
Which fix'd him beyond the power to start.
Though slight was that grasp so mortal cold,
He could not loose him from its hold;   600
But never did clasp of one so dear
Strike on the pulse with such feeling of fear,
As those thin fingers, long and white,
Froze through his blood by their touch that night
The feverish glow of his brow was gone,
And his heart sank so still that it felt like stone,
As he look'd on the face, and beheld its hue,
So deeply changed from what he knew:
Fair but faint—without the ray
Of mind, that made each feature play   610
Like sparkling waves on a sunny day;
And her motionless lips lay still as death,
And her words came forth without her breath,
And there rose not a heave o'er her bosom's swell,

77

And there seem'd not a pulse in her veins to dwell.
Though her eye shone out, yet the lids were fix'd,
And the glance that it gave was wild and unmix'd
With aught of change, as the eyes may seem
Of the restless who walk in a troubled dream;
Like the figures on arras, that gloomily glare,   620
Stirr'd by the breath of the wintry air,
So seen by the dying lamp's fitful light,
Lifeless, but life-like, and awful to sight;
As they seem, through the dimness, about to come down
From the shadowy wall where their images frown;
Fearfully flitting to and fro,
As the gusts on the tapestry come and go.

   'If not for love of me be given
Thus much, then, for the love of heaven,—
Again I say—that turban tear   630
From off thy faithless brow, and swear
Thine injured country's sons to spare,
Or thou art lost; and never shalt see—
Not earth—that's past—but heaven or me.
If this thou dost accord, albeit
A heavy doom 'tis thine to meet,
That doom shall half absolve thy sin,
And mercy's gate may receive thee within:
But pause one moment more, and take
The curse of Him thou didst forsake;   640
And look once more to heaven, and see
Its love for ever shut from thee.
There is a light cloud by the moon—
'Tis passing, and will pass full soon—
If, by the time its vapoury sail
Hath ceased her shaded orb to veil,
Thy heart within thee is not changed,
Then God and man are both avenged;

Dark will thy doom be, darker still
Thine immortality of ill.'   650

Alp look'd to heaven, and saw on high
The sign she spake of in the sky;
But his heart was swollen, and turn'd aside,
By deep interminable pride.
This first false passion of his breast
Roll'd like a torrent o'er the rest.
He sue for mercy! *He* dismay'd
By wild words of a timid maid!
He, wrong'd by Venice, vow to save
Her sons, devoted to the grave!   660
No—though that cloud were thunder's worst,
And charged to crush him—let it burst!

He look'd upon it earnestly,
Without an accent of reply;
He watch'd it passing; it is flown:
Full on his eye the clear moon shone,
And thus he spake—'Whate'er my fate,
I am no changeling—'tis too late:
The reed in storms may bow and quiver,
Then rise again; the tree must shiver.   670
What Venice made me, I must be,
Her foe in all, save love to thee:
But thou art safe: oh, fly with me!'
He turn'd, but she is gone!
Nothing is there but the column stone.
Hath she sunk in the earth, or melted in air?
He saw not—he knew not—but nothing is there.

XXII
The night is past, and shines the sun
As if that morn were a jocund one.

Lightly and brightly breaks away   680
The Morning from her mantle grey,
And the noon will look on a sultry day.
Hark to the trump, and the drum,
And the mournful sound of the barbarous horn,
And the flap of the banners, that flit as they're borne,
And the neigh of the steed, and the multitude's hum,
And the clash, and the shout, 'They come! they come!'
The horsetails are pluck'd from the ground, and the sword
From its sheath; and they form, and but wait for the word.
Tartar, and Spahi, and Turcoman,   690
Strike your tents, and throng to the van;
Mount ye, spur ye, skirr the plain,
That the fugitive may flee in vain,
When he breaks from the town; and none escape,
Aged or young, in the Christian shape;
While your fellows on foot, in a fiery mass,
Bloodstain the breach through which they pass.
The steeds are all bridled, and snort to the rein;
Curved is each neck, and flowing each mane;
White is the foam of their champ on the bit;   700
The spears are uplifted; the matches are lit;
The cannon are pointed, and ready to roar,
And crush the wall they have crumbled before:
Forms in his phalanx each janizar;
Alp at their head; his right arm is bare,
So is the blade of his scimitar;
The khan and the pachas are all at their post;
The vizier himself at the head of the host.
When the culvern's signal is fired, then on;
Leave not in Corinth a living one—   710
A priest at her altars, a chief in her halls,
A hearth in her mansions, a stone on her walls.
God and the prophet—Alla Hu!
Up to the skies with that wild halloo!

'There the breach lies for passage, the ladder to scale;
And your hands on your sabres, and how should ye fail?
He who first downs with the red cross may crave
His heart's dearest wish; let him ask it, and have!'
Thus utter'd Coumourgi, the dauntless vizier;
The reply was the brandish of sabre and spear,   720
And the shout of fierce thousands in joyous ire:—
Silence—hark to the signal—fire!

XXIII

As the wolves, that headlong go
On the stately buffalo,
Though with fiery eyes, and angry roar,
And hoofs that stamp, and horns that gore,
He tramples on earth, or tosses on high
The foremost, who rush on his strength but to die:
Thus against the wall they went,
Thus the first were backward bent;   730
Many a bosom, sheathed in brass,
Strew'd the earth like broken glass,
Shiver'd by the shot, that tore
The ground whereon they moved no more:
Even as they fell, in files they lay,
Like the mower's grass at the close of day,
When his work is done on the levell'd plain;
Such was the fall of the foremost slain.

XXIV

As the spring-tides, with heavy plash,
From the cliffs invading dash   740
Huge fragments, sapp'd by the ceaseless flow,
Till white and thundering down they go,
Like the avalanche's snow
On the Alpine vales below;

Thus at length, outbreathed and worn,
Corinth's sons were downward borne
By the long and oft renew'd
Charge of the Moslem multitude.
In firmness they stood, and in masses they fell,
Heap'd by the host of the infidel,   750
Hand to hand, and foot to foot:
Nothing there, save death, was mute:
Stroke, and thrust, and flash, and cry
For quarter or for victory,
Mingle there with the volleying thunder,
Which makes the distant cities wonder
How the sounding battle goes,
If with them, or for their foes;
If they must mourn, or may rejoice
In that annihilating voice,   760
Which pierces the deep hills through and through
With an echo dread and new:
You might have heard it, on that day,
O'er Salamis and Megara;
(We have heard the hearers say,)
Even unto Piræus' bay.

XXV

From the point of encountering blades to the hilt,
Sabres and swords with blood were gilt;
But the rampart is won, and the spoil begun,
And all but the after carnage done.   770
Shriller shrieks now mingling come
From within the plunder'd dome:
Hark to the haste of flying feet,
That splash in the blood of the slippery street;
But here and there, where 'vantage ground
Against the foe may still be found,
Desperate groups, of twelve or ten,

Make a pause, and turn again—
With banded backs against the wall,
Fiercely stand, or fighting fall.   780

There stood an old man—his hairs were white,
But his veteran arm was full of might:
So gallantly bore he the brunt of the fray,
The dead before him, on that day,
In a semicircle lay;
Still he combated unwounded,
Though retreating, unsurrounded.
Many a scar of former fight
Lurk'd beneath his corslet bright;
But of every wound his body bore,   790
Each and all had been ta'en before:
Though aged, he was so iron of limb,
Few of our youth could cope with him,
And the foes, whom he singly kept at bay,
Outnumber'd his thin hairs of silver grey.
From right to left his sabre swept;
Many an Othman mother wept
Sons that were unborn, when dipp'd
His weapon first in Moslem gore,
Ere his years could count a score.   800
Of all he might have been the sire
Who fell that day beneath his ire:
For, sonless left long years ago,
His wrath made many a childless foe;
And since the day, when in the strait
His only boy had met his fate,
His parent's iron hand did doom
More than a human hecatomb.
If shades by carnage be appeased,
Patroclus' spirit less was pleased   810
Than his, Minotti's son, who died

Where Asia's bounds and ours divide.
Buried he lay, where thousands before
For thousands of years were inhumed on the shore;
What of them is left, to tell
Where they lie, and how they fell?
Not a stone on their turf, nor a bone in their graves;
But they live in the verse that immortally saves.

XXVI

Hark to the Allah shout! a band
Of the Mussulman bravest and best is at hand;   820
Their leader's nervous arm is bare,
Swifter to smite, and never to spare—
Unclothed to the shoulder it waves them on;
Thus in the fight is he ever known:
Others a gaudier garb may show,
To tempt the spoil of the greedy foe;
Many a hand's on a richer hilt,
But none on a steel more ruddily gilt;
Many a loftier turban may wear,—
Alp is but known by the white arm bare;   830
Look through the thick of the fight, 'tis there!
There is not a standard on that shore
So well advanced the ranks before;
There is not a banner in Moslem war
Will lure the Delhis half so far;
It glances like a falling star!
Where'er that mighty arm is seen,
The bravest be, or late have been;
There the craven cries for quarter
Vainly to the vengeful Tartar;   840
Or the hero, silent lying,
Scorns to yield a groan in dying;
Mustering his last feeble blow
'Gainst the nearest levell'd foe,

Though faint beneath the mutual wound,
Grappling on the gory ground.

XXVII
Still the old man stood erect,
And Alp's career a moment check'd.
'Yield thee, Minotti; quarter take,
For thine own, thy daughter's sake.'   850

'Never, renegado, never!
Though the life of thy gift would last for ever.'

'Francesca!—Oh, my promised bride!
Must she too perish by thy pride?'

'She is safe.'—'Where? where?'—'In heaven;
From whence thy traitor soul is driven—
Far from thee, and undefiled.'
Grimly then Minotti smiled,
As he saw Alp staggering bow
Before his words, as with a blow.   860
'Oh God! when died she?'—'Yesternight—
Nor weep I for her spirit's flight:
None of my pure race shall be
Slaves to Mahomet and thee—
Come on!'—That challenge is in vain—
Alp's already with the slain!
While Minotti's words were wreaking
More revenge in bitter speaking
Than his falchion's point had found,
Had the time allow'd to wound,   870
From within the neighbouring porch
Of a long defended church,
Where the last and desperate few
Would the failing fight renew,

The sharp shot dash'd Alp to the ground;
Ere an eye could view the wound
That crash'd through the brain of the infidel,
Round he spun, and down he fell;
A flash like fire within his eyes
Blazed, as he bent no more to rise,   880
And then eternal darkness sunk
Through all the palpitating trunk;
Nought of life left, save a quivering
Where his limbs were slightly shivering:
They turn'd him on his back; his breast
And brow were stain'd with gore and dust,
And through his lips the life-blood oozed,
From its deep veins lately loosed:
But in his pulse there was no throb,
Nor on his lips one dying sob;   890
Sigh, nor word, nor struggling breath
Heralded his way to death;
Ere his very thought could pray,
Unanel'd he pass'd away,
Without a hope from mercy's aid,—
To the last a Renegade.

                          XXVIII
Fearfully the yell arose
Of his followers, and his foes;
These in joy, in fury those:
Then again in conflict mixing,   900
Clashing swords, and spears transfixing,
Interchanged the blow and thrust,
Hurling warriors in the dust.
Street by street, and foot by foot,
Still Minotti dares dispute
The latest portion of the land
Left beneath his high command;

With him, aiding heart and hand,
The remnant of his gallant band.
Still the church is tenable,   910
   Whence issued late the fated ball
   That half avenged the city's fall,
When Alp, her fierce assailant, fell:
Thither bending sternly back,
They leave before a bloody track;
And, with their faces to the foe,
Dealing wounds with every blow,
The chief, and his retreating train,
Join to those within the fane;
There they yet may breathe awhile,   920
Shelter'd by the massy pile.

XXIX

Brief breathing-time! the turban'd host,
With added ranks and raging boast,
Press onwards with such strength and heat,
Their numbers balk their own retreat;
For narrow the way that led to the spot
Where still the Christians yielded not;
And the foremost, if fearful, may vainly try
Through the massy column to turn and fly;
They perforce must do or die.   930
They die; but ere their eyes could close,
Avengers o'er their bodies rose;
Fresh and furious, fast they fill
The ranks unthinn'd, though slaughter'd still;
And faint the weary Christians wax
Before the still renew'd attacks:
And now the Othmans gain the gate;
Still resists its iron weight,
And still, all deadly aim'd and hot,
From every crevice comes the shot;   940

87

From every shatter'd window pour
The volleys of the sulphurous shower:
But the portal wavering grows and weak—
The iron yields, the hinges creak—
It bends—it falls—and all is o'er;
Lost Corinth may resist no more!

XXX

Darkly, sternly, and all alone,
Minotti stood o'er the altar-stone:
Madonna's face upon him shone,
Painted in heavenly hues above.   950
With eyes of light and looks of love;
And placed upon that holy shrine
To fix our thoughts on things divine,
When pictured there, we kneeling see
Her, and the boy-God on her knee,
Smiling sweetly on each prayer
To heaven, as if to waft it there.
Still she smiled; even now she smiles,
Though slaughter streams along her aisles:
Minotti lifted his aged eye,   960
And made the sign of a cross with a sigh,
Then seized a torch which blazed thereby;
And still he stood, while with steel and flame
Inward and onward the Mussulman came.

XXXI

The vaults beneath the mosaic stone
Contain'd the dead of ages gone;
Their names were on the graven floor,
But now illegible with gore;
The carved crests, and curious hues
The varied marble's vein diffuse,   970

88

Were smear'd, and slippery,—stain'd, and strown
With broken swords, and helms o'erthrown:
There were dead above, and the dead below
Lay cold in many a coffin'd row;
You might see them piled in sable state,
By a pale light through a gloomy grate;
But War had enter'd their dark caves,
And stored along the vaulted graves
Her sulphurous treasures, thickly spread
In masses by the fleshless dead: 980
    Here, throughout the siege, had been
    The Christians' chiefest magazine;
To these a late-form'd train now led,
Minotti's last and stern resource
Against the foe's o'erwhelming force.

XXXII

The foe came on, and few remain
To strive, and those must strive in vain:
For lack of further lives, to slake
The thirst of vengeance now awake,
With barbarous blows they gash the dead,   990
And lop the already lifeless head,
And fell the statues from their niche,
And spoil the shrines of offerings rich,
And from each other's rude hands wrest
The silver vessels saints had bless'd.
To the high altar on they go;
Oh, but it made a glorious show!
On its table still behold
The cup of consecrated gold;
Massy and deep, a glittering prize,   1000
Brightly it sparkles to plunderers' eyes:
That morn it held the holy wine,
Converted by Christ to his blood so divine,

89

Which his worshippers drank at the break of day,
To shrive their souls ere they join'd in the fray.
Still a few drops within it lay:
And round the sacred table glow
Twelve lofty lamps, in splendid row,
From the purest metal cast;
A spoil—the richest, and the last.   1010

XXXIII

So near they came, the nearest stretch'd
To grasp the spoil he almost reach'd,
  When old Minotti's hand
Touch'd with the torch the train—
  'Tis fired!
Spire, vaults, the shrine, the spoil, the slain,
  The turban'd victors, the Christian band,
All that of living or dead remain,
Hurl'd on high with the shiver'd fane,
  In one wild roar expired!   1020
The shatter'd town—the walls thrown down—
The waves a moment backward bent—
The hills that shake, although unrent,
  As if an earthquake pass'd—
The thousand shapeless things all driven
In cloud and flame athwart the heaven,
  By that tremendous blast—
Proclaim'd the desperate conflict o'er
On that too long afflicted shore:
Up to the sky like rockets go   1030
All that mingled there below:
Many a tall and goodly man,
Scorch'd and shrivell'd to a span,
When he fell to earth again
Like a cinder strew'd the plain:
Down the ashes shower like rain;

Some fell in the gulf, which received the sprinkles
With a thousand circling wrinkles;
Some fell on the shore, but, far away,
Scatter'd o'er the isthmus lay;   1040
Christian or Moslem, which be they?
Let their mothers see and say!
When in cradled rest they lay,
And each nursing mother smiled
On the sweet sleep of her child,
Little deem'd she such a day
Would rend those tender limbs away.
Not the matrons that them bore
Could discern their offspring more;
That one moment left no trace   1050
More of human form or face
Save a scatter'd scalp or bone:
And down came blazing rafters, strown
Around, and many a falling stone,
Deeply dinted in the clay,
All blacken'd there and reeking lay.
All the living things that heard
That deadly earth-shock disappear'd:
The wild birds flew; the wild dogs fled,
And howling left the unburied dead;   1060
The camels from their keepers broke;
The distant steer forsook the yoke—
The nearer steed plunged o'er the plain,
And burst his girth, and tore his rein;
The bull-frog's note, from out the marsh,
Deep-mouth'd arose, and doubly harsh;
The wolves yell'd on the cavern'd hill
Where echo roll'd in thunder still;
The jackals' troop, in gather'd cry,
Bay'd from afar complainingly,   1070
With a mix'd and mournful sound,

Like crying babe, and beaten hound:
With sudden wing, and ruffled breast,
The eagle left his rocky nest,
And mounted nearer to the sun,
The clouds beneath him seem'd so dun;
Their smoke assail'd his startled beak,
And made him higher soar and shriek—
      Thus was Corinth lost and won!

The Prisoner of Chillon

My hair is grey, but not with years,
      Nor grew it white
      In a single night,
As men's have grown from sudden fears:
My limbs are bow'd, though not with toil,
   But rusted with a vile repose,
For they have been a dungeon's spoil,
   And mine has been the fate of those
To whom the goodly earth and air
Are bann'd, and barr'd—forbidden fare: 10
But this was for my father's faith
I suffer'd chains and courted death;
That father perish'd at the stake
For tenets he would not forsake;
And for the same his lineal race
In darkness found a dwelling-place;
We were seven—who now are one,
      Six in youth, and one in age,
Finish'd as they had begun,
      Proud of Persecution's rage;   20

One in fire, and two in field,
Their belief with blood have seal'd,
Dying as their father died,
For the God their foes denied;
Three were in a dungeon cast,
Of whom this wreck is left the last.

II

There are seven pillars of Gothic mould
In Chillon's dungeons deep and old,
There are seven columns, massy and grey,
Dim with a dull imprison'd ray,   30
A sunbeam which hath lost its way,
And through the crevice and the cleft
Of the thick wall is fallen and left;
Creeping o'er the floor so damp,
Like a marsh's meteor lamp:
And in each pillar there is a ring,
   And in each ring there is a chain;
That iron is a cankering thing,
   For in these limbs its teeth remain,
With marks that will not wear away,   40
Till I have done with this new day,
Which now is painful to these eyes,
Which have not seen the sun so rise
For years—I cannot count them o'er,
I lost their long and heavy score,
When my last brother droop'd and died,
And I lay living by his side.

III

They chain'd us each to a column stone,
And we were three—yet, each alone;
We could not move a single pace,   50
We could not see each other's face,

But with that pale and livid light
   That made us strangers in our sight:
And thus together—yet apart,
Fetter'd in hand, but join'd in heart,
'Twas still some solace, in the dearth
Of the pure elements of earth,
To hearken to each other's speech,
And each turn comforter to each
With some new hope, or legend old,   60
Or song heroically bold;
But even these at length grew cold.
Our voices took a dreary tone,
An echo of the dungeon stone,
   A grating sound, not full and free,
   As they of yore were wont to be:
   It might be fancy, but to me
They never sounded like our own.

IV

I was the eldest of the three,
   And to uphold and cheer the rest   70
   I ought to do—and did my best—
And each did well in his degree.
   The youngest, whom my father loved,
Because our mother's brow was given
To him, with eyes as blue as heaven—
   For him my soul was sorely moved;
And truly might it be distress'd
To see such bird in such a nest;
For he was beautiful as day—
   (When day was beautiful to me   80
   As to young eagles, being free)—
   A polar day, which will not see
A sunset till its summer's gone,
   Its sleepless summer of long light,

The snow-clad offspring of the sun:
  And thus he was as pure and bright,
And in his natural spirit gay,
With tears for nought but others' ills,
And then they flow'd like mountain rills,
Unless he could assuage the woe   90
Which he abhorr'd to view below.

v

The other was as pure of mind,
But form'd to combat with his kind;
Strong in his frame, and of a mood
Which 'gainst the world in war had stood,
And perish'd in the foremost rank
  With joy:—but not in chains to pine:
His spirit wither'd with their clank,
  I saw it silently decline—
  And so perchance in sooth did mine: 100
But yet I forced it on to cheer
Those relics of a home so dear.
He was a hunter of the hills,
  Had follow'd there the deer and wolf;
  To him his dungeon was a gulf,
And fetter'd feet the worst of ills.

VI

  Lake Leman lies by Chillon's walls:
A thousand feet in depth below
Its massy waters meet and flow;
Thus much the fathom-line was sent   110
From Chillon's snow-white battlement,
  Which round about the wave inthrals:
A double dungeon wall and wave
Have made—and like a living grave
Below the surface of the lake

95

The dark vault lies wherein we lay,
We heard it ripple night and day;
   Sounding o'er our heads it knock'd;
And I have felt the winter's spray
Wash through the bars when winds were high   120
And wanton in the happy sky;
   And then the very rock hath rock'd,
   And I have felt it shake, unshock'd,
Because I could have smiled to see
The death that would have set me free.

VII

I said my nearer brother pined,
I said his mighty heart declined,
He loathed and put away his food;
It was not that 'twas coarse and rude,
For we were used to hunter's fare,   130
And for the like had little care:
The milk drawn from the mountain goat
Was changed for water from the moat,
Our bread was such as captives' tears
Have moisten'd many a thousand years,
Since man first pent his fellow men
Like brutes within an iron den;
But what were these to us or him?
These wasted not his heart or limb;
My brother's soul was of that mould   140
Which in a palace had grown cold,
Had his free breathing been denied
The range of the steep mountain's side;
But why delay the truth?—he died.
I saw, and could not hold his head,
Nor reach his dying hand—nor dead,—
Though hard I strove, but strove in vain,
To rend and gnash my bonds in twain.

He died, and they unlock'd his chain,
And scoop'd for him a shallow grave   150
Even from the cold earth of our cave.
I begg'd them as a boon to lay
His corse in dust whereon the day
Might shine—it was a foolish thought,
But then within my brain it wrought,
That even in death his freeborn breast
In such a dungeon could not rest.
I might have spared my idle prayer—
They coldly laugh'd, and laid him there:
The flat and turfless earth above   160
The being we so much did love;
His empty chain above it leant,
Such murder's fitting monument!

VIII

But he, the favourite and the flower,
Most cherish'd since his natal hour,
His mother's image in fair face,
The infant love of all his race,
His martyr'd father's dearest thought,
My latest care, for whom I sought
To hoard my life, that his might be   170
Less wretched now, and one day free;
He, too, who yet had held untired
A spirit natural or inspired—
He, too, was struck, and day by day
Was wither'd on the stalk away.
Oh, God! it is a fearful thing
To see the human soul take wing
In any shape, in any mood:
I've seen it rushing forth in blood,
I've seen it on the breaking ocean   180
Strive with a swoln convulsive motion,

97

I've seen the sick and ghastly bed
Of Sin delirious with its dread;
But these were horrors—this was woe
Unmix'd with such—but sure and slow:
He faded, and so calm and meek,
So softly worn, so sweetly weak,
So tearless, yet so tender, kind,
And grieved for those he left behind;
With all the while a cheek whose bloom   190
Was as a mockery of the tomb,
Whose tints as gently sunk away
As a departing rainbow's ray;
An eye of most transparent light,
That almost made the dungeon bright,
And not a word of murmur, not
A groan o'er his untimely lot,—
A little talk of better days,
A little hope my own to raise,
For I was sunk in silence—lost   200
In this last loss, of all the most;
And then the sighs he would suppress
Of fainting nature's feebleness,
More slowly drawn, grew less and less:
I listen'd, but I could not hear;
I call'd, for I was wild with fear;
I knew 'twas hopeless, but my dread
Would not be thus admonished;
I call'd, and thought I heard a sound—
I burst my chain with one strong bound,   210
And rush'd to him:—I found him not,
I only stirr'd in this black spot,
I only lived, *I* only drew
The accursed breath of dungeon-dew;
The last, the sole, the dearest link
Between me and the eternal brink,

Which bound me to my failing race,
Was broken in this fatal place.
One on the earth, and one beneath—
My brothers—both had ceased to breathe: 220
I took that hand which lay so still,
Alas! my own was full as chill;
I had not strength to stir, or strive,
But felt that I was still alive—
A frantic feeling, when we know
That what we love shall ne'er be so.
    I know not why
    I could not die,
I had no earthly hope but faith,
And that forbade a selfish death.   230

IX

What next befell me then and there
   I know not well—I never knew—
First came the loss of light, and air,
   And then of darkness too:
I had no thought, no feeling—none—
Among the stones I stood a stone,
And was, scarce conscious what I wist,
As shrubless crags within the mist;
For all was blank, and bleak, and grey;
It was not night, it was not day;   240
It was not even the dungeon-light,
So hateful to my heavy sight,
But vacancy absorbing space,
And fixedness without a place;
There were no stars, no earth, no time,
No check, no change, no good, no crime,
But silence, and a stirless breath
Which neither was of life nor death;

A sea of stagnant idleness,
Blind, boundless, mute, and motionless! 250

X

A light broke in upon my brain,—
   It was the carol of a bird;
It ceased, and then it came again,
   The sweetest song ear ever heard,
And mine was thankful till my eyes
Ran over with the glad surprise,
And they that moment could not see
I was the mate of misery;
But then by dull degrees came back
My senses to their wonted track; 260
I saw the dungeon walls and floor
Close slowly round me as before,
I saw the glimmer of the sun
Creeping as it before had done,
But through the crevice where it came
That bird was perch'd, as fond and tame,
   And tamer than upon the tree;
A lovely bird, with azure wings,
And song that said a thousand things,
   And seem'd to say them all for me! 270
I never saw its like before,
I ne'er shall see its likeness more:
It seem'd like me to want a mate,
But was not half so desolate,
And it was come to love me when
None lived to love me so again,
And cheering from my dungeon's brink,
Had brought me back to feel and think.
I know not if it late were free,
   Or broke its cage to perch on mine, 280

But knowing well captivity,
   Sweet bird! I could not wish for thine!
Or if it were, in winged guise,
A visitant from Paradise;
For—Heaven forgive that thought! the while
Which made me both to weep and smile—
I sometimes deem'd that it might be
My brother's soul come down to me;
But then at last away it flew,
And then 'twas mortal well I knew,   290
For he would never thus have flown,
And left me twice so doubly lone,
Lone as the corse within its shroud,
Lone as a solitary cloud,—
   A single cloud on a sunny day,
While all the rest of heaven is clear,
A frown upon the atmosphere,
That hath no business to appear
   When skies are blue, and earth is gay.

XI

A kind of change came in my fate,   300
My keepers grew compassionate;
I know not what had made them so,
They were inured to sights of woe,
But so it was:—my broken chain
With links unfasten'd did remain,
And it was liberty to stride
Along my cell from side to side,
And up and down, and then athwart,
And tread it over every part;
And round the pillars one by one,   310
Returning where my walk begun,
Avoiding only, as I trod,
My brothers' graves without a sod;

For if I thought with heedless tread
My step profaned their lowly bed,
My breath came gaspingly and thick,
And my crush'd heart felt blind and sick.

XII

I made a footing in the wall,
   It was not therefrom to escape,
For I had buried one and all   320
   Who loved me in a human shape;
And the whole earth would henceforth be
A wider prison unto me:
No child, no sire, no kin had I,
No partner in my misery;
I thought of this, and I was glad,
For thought of them had made me mad;
But I was curious to ascend
To my barr'd windows, and to bend
Once more upon the mountains high,   330
The quiet of a loving eye.

XIII

I saw them, and they were the same,
They were not changed like me in frame;
I saw their thousand years of snow
On high—their wide long lake below,
And the blue Rhone in fullest flow;
I heard the torrents leap and gush
O'er channell'd rock and broken bush;
I saw the white-wall'd distant town,
And whiter sails go skimming down;   340
And then there was a little isle,
Which in my very face did smile,
     The only one in view;

102

A small green isle, it seem'd no more,
Scarce broader than my dungeon floor,
But in it there were three tall trees,
And o'er it blew the mountain breeze,
And by it there were waters flowing,
And on it there were young flowers growing,
    Of gentle breath and hue.   350
The fish swam by the castle wall,
And they seem'd joyous each and all;
The eagle rode the rising blast,
Methought he never flew so fast
As then to me he seem'd to fly;
And then new tears came in my eye,
And I felt troubled—and would fain
I had not left my recent chain;
And when I did descend again,
The darkness of my dim abode   360
Fell on me as a heavy load;
It was as is a new-dug grave,
Closing o'er one we sought to save,—
And yet my glance, too much opprest,
Had almost need of such a rest.

XIV

It might be months, or years, or days,
    I kept no count, I took no note,
I had no hope my eyes to raise,
    And clear them of their dreary mote;
At last men came to set me free;   370
    I ask'd not why, and reck'd not where;
It was at length the same to me,
Fetter'd or fetterless to be,
    I learn'd to love despair.
And thus when they appear'd at last,
And all my bonds aside were cast,

These heavy walls to me had grown
A hermitage—and all my own!
And half I felt as they were come
To tear me from a second home: 380
With spiders I had friendship made,
And watch'd them in their sullen trade,
Had seen the mice by moonlight play,
And why should I feel less than they?
We were all inmates of one place,
And I, the monarch of each race,
Had power to kill—yet, strange to tell!
In quiet we had learn'd to dwell;
My very chains and I grew friends,
So much a long communion tends   390
To make us what we are:—even I
Regain'd my freedom with a sigh

The Vision of Judgment

I

Saint Peter sat by the celestial gate:
    His keys were rusty, and the lock was dull,
So little trouble had been given of late;
    Not that the place by any means was full,
But since the Gallic era 'eighty-eight'
    The devils had ta'en a longer, stronger pull,
And 'a pull altogether,' as they say
At sea—which drew most souls another way.

II

The angels all were singing out of tune,
    And hoarse with having little else to do,   10

Excepting to wind up the sun and moon,
  Or curb a runaway young star or two,
Or wild colt of a comet, which too soon
  Broke out of bounds o'er th' ethereal blue,
Splitting some planet with its playful tail,
  As boats are sometimes by a wanton whale.

III

The guardian seraphs had retired on high,
  Finding their charges past all care below;
Terrestrial business fill'd nought in the sky
  Save the recording angel's black bureau;   20
Who found, indeed, the facts to multiply
  With such rapidity of vice and woe,
That he had stripp'd off both his wings in quills,
And yet was in arrear of human ills.

IV

His business so augmented of late years,
  That he was forced, against his will no doubt,
(Just like those cherubs, earthly ministers,)
  For some resource to turn himself about,
And claim the help of his celestial peers,
  To aid him ere he should be quite worn out   30
By the increased demand for his remarks:
Six angels and twelve saints were named his clerks.

V

This was a handsome board—at least for heaven;
  And yet they had even then enough to do,
So many conquerors' cars were daily driven,
  So many kingdoms fitted up anew;
Each day too slew its thousands six or seven,
  Till at the crowning carnage, Waterloo,
They threw their pens down in divine disgust—
The page was so besmear'd with blood and dust.   40

VI

This by the way; 'tis not mine to record
  What angels shrink from: even the very devil
On this occasion his own work abhorr'd,
  So surfeited with the infernal revel:
Though he himself had sharpen'd every sword,
  It almost quench'd his innate thirst of evil.
(Here Satan's sole good work deserves insertion—
'Tis, that he has both generals in reversion.)

VII

Let's skip a few short years of hollow peace,
  Which peopled earth no better, hell as wont,   50
And heaven none—they form the tyrant's lease,
  With nothing but new names subscribed upon't;
'Twill one day finish: meantime they increase,
  'With seven heads and ten horns,' and all in front,
Like Saint John's foretold beast; but ours are born
Less formidable in the head than horn.

VIII

In the first year of freedom's second dawn
  Died George the Third; although no tyrant, one
Who shielded tyrants, till each sense withdrawn
  Left him nor mental nor external sun: 60
A better farmer ne'er brush'd dew from lawn,
  A worse king never left a realm undone!
He died—but left his subjects still behind,
One half as mad—and t'other no less blind.

IX

He died! his death made no great stir on earth:
  His burial made some pomp; there was profusion
Of velvet, gilding, brass, and no great dearth
  Of aught but tears—save those shed by collusion.

For these things may be bought at their true worth;
   Of elegy there was the due infusion—   70
Bought also; and the torches, cloaks, and banners,
Heralds, and relics of old Gothic manners,

X

Form'd a sepulchral melodrame. Of all
   The fools who flock'd to swell or see the show,
Who cared about the corpse? The funeral
   Made the attraction, and the black the woe.
There throbb'd not there a thought which pierced the pall;
   And when the gorgeous coffin was laid low,
It seem'd the mockery of hell to fold
The rottenness of eighty years in gold.   80

XI

So mix his body with the dust! It might
   Return to what it *must* far sooner, were
The natural compound left alone to fight
   Its way back into earth, and fire, and air;
But the unnatural balsams merely blight
   What nature made him at his birth, as bare
As the mere million's base unmummied clay—
Yet all his spices but prolong decay.

XII

He's dead—and upper earth with him has done;
   He's buried; save the undertaker's bill,   90
Or lapidary scrawl, the world is gone
   For him, unless he left a German will:
But where's the proctor who will ask his son?
   In whom his qualities are reigning still,
Except that household virtue, most uncommon,
Of constancy to a bad, ugly woman.

XIII

'God save the king!' It is a large economy
  In God to save the like; but if he will
Be saving, all the better; for not one am I
  Of those who think damnation better still;   100
I hardly know too if not quite alone am I
  In this small hope of bettering future ill
By circumscribing, with some slight restriction,
The eternity of hell's hot jurisdiction.

XIV

I know this is unpopular; I know
  'Tis blasphemous; I know one may be damn'd
For hoping no one else may e'er be so;
  I know my catechism; I know we're cramm'd
With the best doctrines till we quite o'erflow;
  I know that all save England's church have shamm'd,   110
And that the other twice two hundred churches
And synagogues have made a *damn'd* bad purchase.

XV

God help us all! God help me too! I am,
  God knows, as helpless as the devil can wish,
And not a whit more difficult to damn,
  Than is to bring to land a late-hook'd fish,
Or to the butcher to purvey the lamb;
  Not that I'm fit for such a noble dish,
As one day will be that immortal fry
Of almost everybody born to die.   120

XVI

Saint Peter sat by the celestial gate,
  And nodded o'er his keys; when, lo! there came
A wondrous noise he had not heard of late—
  A rushing sound of wind, and stream and flame;

In short, a roar of things extremely great,
    Which would have made aught save a saint exclaim;
But he, with first a start and then a wink,
Said, 'There's another star gone out, I think!'

XVII

But ere he could return to his repose,
    A cherub flapp'd his right wing o'er his eyes—   130
At which Saint Peter yawn'd, and rubb'd his nose:
    'Saint porter,' said the angel, 'prithee rise!'
Waving a goodly wing, which glow'd, as glows
    An earthly peacock's tail, with heavenly dyes:
To which the saint replied, 'Well, what's the matter?
Is Lucifer come back with all this clatter?'

XVIII

'No,' quoth the cherub; 'George the Third is dead.'
    'And who *is* George the Third?' replied the apostle:
'*What George? what Third?*' 'The king of England,' said
    The angel. 'Well! he won't find kings to jostle   140
Him on his way; but does he wear his head?
    Because the last we saw here had a tustle,
And ne'er would have got into heaven's good graces,
Had he not flung his head in all our faces.

XIX

'He was, if I remember, king of France;
    That head of his, which could not keep a crown
On earth, yet ventured in my face to advance
    A claim to those of martyrs—like my own:
If I had had my sword, as I had once
    When I cut ears off, I had cut him down;   150
But having but my *keys*, and not my brand,
I only knock'd his head from out his hand.

109

XX

'And then he set up such a headless howl,
  That all the saints came out and took him in;
And there he sits by St. Paul, cheek by jowl;
  That fellow Paul—the parvenù! The skin
Of St. Bartholomew, which makes his cowl
  In heaven, and upon earth redeem'd his sin,
So as to make a martyr, never sped
Better than did this weak and wooden head.   160

XXI

'But had it come up here upon its shoulders,
  There would have been a different tale to tell:
The fellow-feeling in the saint's beholders
  Seems to have acted on them like a spell,
And so this very foolish head heaven solders
  Back on its trunk: it may be very well,
And seems the custom here to overthrow
Whatever has been wisely done below.'

XXII

The angel answer'd, 'Peter! do not pout:
  The king who comes has head and all entire,   170
And never knew much what it was about—
  He did as doth the puppet—by its wire,
And will be judged like all the rest, no doubt:
  My business and your own is not to inquire
Into such matters, but to mind our cue—
  Which is to act as we are bid to do.'

XXIII

While thus they spake, the angelic caravan,
  Arriving like a rush of mighty wind,
Cleaving the fields of space, as doth the swan
  Some silver stream (say Ganges, Nile, or Inde,   180

Or Thames, or Tweed), and 'midst them an old man
    With an old soul, and both extremely blind,
Halted before the gate, and in his shroud
Seated their fellow traveller on a cloud.

XXIV

But bringing up the rear of this bright host
    A spirit of a different aspect waved
His wings, like thunder-clouds above some coast
    Whose barren beach with frequent wrecks is paved;
His brow was like the deep when tempest-toss'd;
    Fierce and unfathomable thoughts engraved   190
Eternal wrath on his immortal face,
And *where* he gazed a gloom pervaded space.

XXV

As he drew near, he gazed upon the gate
    Ne'er to be enter'd more by him or Sin,
With such a glance of supernatural hate,
    As made Saint Peter wish himself within;
He patter'd with his keys at a great rate,
    And sweated through his apostolic skin:
Of course his perspiration was but ichor,
Or some such other spiritual liquor.   200

XXVI

The very cherubs huddled all together,
    Like birds when soars the falcon; and they felt
A tingling to the tip of every feather,
    And form'd a circle like Orion's belt
Around their poor old charge; who scarce knew whither
    His guards had led him, though they gently dealt
With royal manes (for by many stories,
And true, we learn the angels all are Tories).

III

XXVII

As things were in this posture, the gate flew
  Asunder, and the flashing of its hinges   210
Flung over space an universal hue
  Of many-colour'd flame, until its tinges
Reach'd even our speck of earth, and made a new
  Aurora borealis spread its fringes
O'er the North Pole; the same seen, when ice-bound,
By Captain Parry's crew, in 'Melville's Sound.'

XXVIII

And from the gate thrown open issued beaming
  A beautiful and mighty Thing of Light,
Radiant with glory, like a banner streaming
  Victorious from some world-o'erthrowing fight: 220
My poor comparisons must needs be teeming
  With earthly likenesses, for here the night
Of clay obscures our best conceptions, saving
Johanna Southcote, or Bob Southey raving.

XXIX

'Twas the archangel Michael; all men know
  The make of angels and archangels, since
There's scarce a scribbler has not one to show,
  From the fiends' leader to the angels' prince;
There also are some altar-pieces, though
  I really can't say that they much evince   230
One's inner notions of immortal spirits;
But let the connoisseurs explain *their* merits.

XXX

Michael flew forth in glory and in good;
  A goodly work of him from whom all glory
And good arise; the portal past—he stood;
  Before him the young cherubs and saints hoary—

(I say *young*, begging to be understood
   By looks, not years; and should be very sorry
To state, they were not older than St. Peter,
But merely that they seem'd a little sweeter).   240

XXXI

The cherubs and the saints bow'd down before
   That arch-angelic hierarch, the first
Of essences angelical, who wore
   The aspect of a god; but this ne'er nursed
Pride in his heavenly bosom, in whose core
   No thought, save for his Master's service, durst
Intrude, however glorified and high;
He knew him but the viceroy of the sky.

XXXII

He and the sombre, silent Spirit met—
   They knew each other both for good and ill;   250
Such was their power, that neither could forget
   His former friend and future foe; but still
There was a high, immortal, proud regret
   In either's eye, as if 'twere less their will
Than destiny to make the eternal years
Their date of war, and their 'champ clos' the spheres.

XXXIII

But here they were in neutral space: we know
   From Job, that Satan hath the power to pay
A heavenly visit thrice a year or so;
   And that the 'sons of God', like those of clay,   260
Must keep him company; and we might show
   From the same book, in how polite a way
The dialogue is held between the Powers
Of Good and Evil—but 'twould take up hours.

113

XXXIV

And this is not a theologic tract,
    To prove with Hebrew and with Arabic,
If Job be allegory or a fact,
    But a true narrative; and thus I pick
From out the whole but such and such an act
    As sets aside the slightest thought of trick.   270
'Tis every tittle true, beyond suspicion,
And accurate as any other vision.

The spirits were in neutral space, before
    The gate of heaven; like eastern thresholds is
The place where Death's grand cause is argued o'er,
    And souls despatch'd to that world or to this;
And therefore Michael and the other wore
    A civil aspect: though they did not kiss,
Yet still between his Darkness and his Brightness
There pass'd a mutual glance of great politeness.   280

XXXVI

The Archangel bow'd, not like a modern beau,
    But with a graceful Oriental bend,
Pressing one radiant arm just where below
    The heart in good men is supposed to tend;
He turn'd as to an equal, not too low,
    But kindly; Satan met his ancient friend
With more hauteur, as might an old Castilian
Poor noble meet a mushroom rich civilian.

He merely bent his diabolic brow
    An instant; and then raising it, he stood   290
In act to assert his right or wrong, and show
    Cause why King George by no means could or should

Make out a case to be exempt from woe
   Eternal, more than other kings, endued
With better sense and hearts, whom history mentions,
Who long have 'paved hell with their good intentions.'

XXXVIII

Michael began: 'What wouldst thou with this man,
   Now dead, and brought before the Lord? What ill
Hath he wrought since his mortal race began,
   That thou canst claim him? Speak! and do thy will,   300
If it be just: if in this earthly span
   He hath been greatly failing to fulfil
His duties as a king and mortal, say,
And he is thine; if not, let him have way.'

XXXIX

'Michael!' replied the Prince of Air, 'even here,
   Before the Gate of him thou servest, must
I claim my subject: and will make appear
   That as he was my worshipper in dust,
So shall he be in spirit, although dear
   To thee and thine, because nor wine nor lust   310
Were of his weaknesses; yet on the throne
He reign'd o'er millions to serve me alone.

XL

'Look to *our* earth, or rather *mine; it* was,
   Once, more thy master's: but I triumph not
In this poor planet's conquest; nor, alas!
   Need he thou servest envy me my lot:
With all the myriads of bright worlds which pass
   In worship round him, he may have forgot
Yon weak creation of such paltry things:
I think few worth damnation save their kings,—   320

115

XLI

'And these but as a kind of quit-rent, to
   Assert my right as lord: and even had
I such an inclination, 'twere (as you
   Well know) superfluous; they are grown so bad,
That hell has nothing better left to do
   Than leave them to themselves: so much more mad
And evil by their own internal curse,
Heaven cannot make them better, nor I worse.

'Look to the earth, I said, and say again:
   When this old, blind, mad, helpless, weak, poor worm   330
Began in youth's first bloom and flush to reign,
   The world and he both wore a different form,
And much of earth and all the watery plain
   Of ocean call'd him king: through many a storm
His isles had floated on the abyss of time;
For the rough virtues chose them for their clime.

XLIII

'He came to his sceptre young; he leaves it old:
   Look to the state in which he found his realm,
And left it; and his annals too behold,
   How to a minion first he gave the helm;   340
How grew upon his heart a thirst for gold,
   The beggar's vice, which can but overwhelm
The meanest hearts; and for the rest, but glance
Thine eye along America and France.

''Tis true, he was a tool from first to last
   (I have the workmen safe); but as a tool
So let him be consumed. From out the past
   Of ages, since mankind have known the rule

Of monarchs—from the bloody rolls amass'd
  Of sin and slaughter—from the Cæsar's school,   350
Take the worst pupil; and produce a reign
More drench'd with gore, more cumber'd with the slain.

XLV

'He ever warr'd with freedom and the free:
  Nations as men, home subjects, foreign foes,
So that they utter'd the word "Liberty!"
  Found George the Third their first opponent. Whose
History was ever stain'd as his will be
  With national and individual woes?
I grant his household abstinence; I grant
His neutral virtues, which most monarchs want;   360

XLVI

'I know he was a constant consort; own
  He was a decent sire, and middling lord.
All this is much, and most upon a throne;
  As temperance, if at Apicius' board,
Is more than at an anchorite's supper shown.
  I grant him all the kindest can accord;
And this was well for him, but not for those
Millions who found him what oppression chose.

XLVII

'The New World shook him off; the Old yet groans
  Beneath what he and his prepared, if not   370
Completed: he leaves heirs on many thrones
  To all his vices, without what begot
Compassion for him—his tame virtues; drones
  Who sleep, or despots who have now forgot
A lesson which shall be re-taught them, wake
Upon the thrones of earth; but let them quake!

XLVIII

'Five millions of the primitive, who hold
   The faith which makes ye great on earth, implored
A *part* of that vast *all* they held of old,—
   Freedom to worship—not alone your Lord,   380
Michael, but you, and you, Saint Peter! Cold
   Must be your souls, if you have not abhorr'd
The foe to Catholic participation
In all the license of a Christian nation.

XLIX

'True! he allow'd them to pray God; but as
   A consequence of prayer, refused the law
Which would have placed them upon the same base
   With those who did not hold the saints in awe.'
But here Saint Peter started from his place,
   And cried, 'You may the prisoner withdraw: 390
Ere heaven shall ope her portals to this Guelph,
While I am guard, may I be damn'd myself?

L

'Sooner will I with Cerberus exchange
   My office (and *his* is no sinecure)
Than see this royal Bedlam bigot range
   The azure fields of heaven, of that be sure!'
'Saint!' replied Satan, 'you do well to avenge
   The wrongs he made your satellites endure;
And if to this exchange you should be given,
I'll try to coax *our* Cerberus up to heaven!'   400

LI

Here Michael interposed: 'Good saint! and devil!
   Pray, not so fast; you both outrun discretion.
Saint Peter! you were wont to be more civil!
   Satan! excuse this warmth of his expression,

And condescension to the vulgar's level:
Even saints sometimes forget themselves in session.
Have you got more to say?'—'No.'—'If you please,
I'll trouble you to call your witnesses.'

LII

Then Satan turn'd and waved his swarthy hand,
  Which stirr'd with its electric qualities   410
Clouds farther off than we can understand,
  Although we find him sometimes in our skies;
Infernal thunder shook both sea and land
  In all the planets, and hell's batteries
Let off the artillery, which Milton mentions
As one of Satan's most sublime inventions.

LIII

This was a signal unto such damn'd souls
  As have the privilege of their damnation
Extended far beyond the mere controls
  Of worlds past, present, or to come; no station   420
Is theirs particularly in the rolls
  Of hell assign'd; but where their inclination
Or business carries them in search of game,
They may range freely—being damn'd the same.

LIV

They're proud of this—as very well they may,
  It being a sort of knighthood, or gilt key
Stuck in their loins; or like to an 'entré'
  Up the back stairs, or such freemasonry.
I borrow my comparisons from clay,
  Being clay myself. Let not those spirits be   430
Offended with such base low likenesses;
We know their posts are nobler far than these.

LV

When the great signal ran from heaven to hell—
   About ten million times the distance reckon'd
From our sun to its earth, as we can tell
   How much time it takes up, even to a second,
For every ray that travels to dispel
   The fogs of London, through which, dimly beacon'd,
The weathercocks are gilt some thrice a year,
If that the *summer* is not too severe: 440

LVI

I say that I can tell—'twas half a minute;
   I know the solar beams take up more time
Ere, pack'd up for their journey, they begin it;
   But then their telegraph is less sublime,
And if they ran a race, they would not win it
   'Gainst Satan's couriers bound for their own clime.
The sun takes up some years for every ray
To reach its goal—the devil not half a day.

LVII

Upon the verge of space, about the size
   Of half-a-crown, a little speck appear'd   450
(I've seen a something like it in the skies
   In the Ægean, ere a squall); it near'd,
And, growing bigger, took another guise;
   Like an aërial ship it tack'd, and steer'd,
Or *was* steer'd (I am doubtful of the grammar
Of the last phrase, which makes the stanza stammer;—

LVIII

But take your choice): and then it grew a cloud;
   And so it was—a cloud of witnesses.
But such a cloud! No land e'er saw a crowd
   Of locusts numerous as the heavens saw these;   460

They shadow'd with their myriads space; their loud
   And varied cries were like those of wild geese
(If nations may be liken'd to a goose),
And realised the phrase of 'hell broke loose.'

LIX

Here crash'd a sturdy oath of stout John Bull,
   Who damn'd away his eyes as heretofore:
There Paddy brogued 'By Jasus!'—'What's your wull?'
The temperate Scot exclaim'd: the French ghost swore
In certain terms I shan't translate in full,
   As the first coachman will; and 'midst the war,   470
The voice of Jonathan was heard to express,
'*Our* president is going to war, I guess.'

LX

Besides there were the Spaniard, Dutch, and Dane;
   In short, an universal shoal of shades,
From Otaheite's isle to Salisbury Plain,
   Of all climes and professions, years and trades,
Ready to swear against the good king's reign,
   Bitter as clubs in cards are against spades:
All summon'd by this grand 'subpœna,' to
Try if kings mayn't be damn'd like me or you.   480

LXI

When Michael saw this host, he first grew pale,
   As angels can; next, like Italian twilight,
He turn'd all colours—as a peacock's tail,
   Or sunset streaming through a Gothic skylight
In some old abbey, or a trout not stale,
   Or distant lightning on the horizon *by* night,
Or a fresh rainbow, or a grand review
Of thirty regiments in red, green, and blue.

LXII

Then he address'd himself to Satan: 'Why—
  My good old friend, for such I deem you, though   490
Our different parties make us fight so shy,
  I ne'er mistake you for a *personal* foe;
Our difference is *political*, and I
  Trust that, whatever may occur below,
You know my great respect for you: and this
Makes me regret whate'er you do amiss—

LXIII

'Why, my dear Lucifer, would you abuse
  My call for witnesses? I did not mean
That you should half of earth and hell produce;
  'Tis even superfluous, since two honest, clean,   500
True testimonies are enough: we lose
  Our time, nay, our eternity, between
The accusation and defence: if we
Hear both, 'twill stretch our immortality.'

LXIV

Satan replied, 'To me the matter is
  Indifferent, in a personal point of view:
I can have fifty better souls than this
  With far less trouble than we have gone through
Already; and I merely argued his
  Late majesty of Britain's case with you   510
Upon a point of form: you may dispose
Of him; I've kings enough below, God knows!'

LXV

Thus spoke the Demon (late call'd 'multi-faced'
  By multo-scribbling Southey). 'Then we'll call
One or two persons of the myriads placed
  Around our congress, and dispense with all

The rest,' quoth Michael: 'Who may be so graced
   As to speak first? there's choice enough—who shall
It be?' Then Satan answer'd, 'There are many;
But you may choose Jack Wilkes as well as any.'   520

LXVI

A merry, cock-eyed, curious-looking sprite
   Upon the instant started from the throng,
Dress'd in a fashion now forgotten quite;
   For all the fashions of the flesh stick long
By people in the next world; where unite
   All the costumes since Adam's, right or wrong,
From Eve's fig-leaf down to the petticoat,
Almost as scanty, of days less remote.

LXVII

The spirit look'd around upon the crowds
   Assembled, and exclaim'd, 'My friends of all   530
The spheres, we shall catch cold amongst these clouds;
   So let's to business: why this general call?
If those are freeholders I see in shrouds,
   And 'tis for an election that they bawl,
Behold a candidate with unturn'd coat!
Saint Peter, may I count upon your vote?'

LXVIII

'Sir,' replied Michael, 'you mistake; these things
   Are of a former life, and what we do
Above is more august; to judge of kings
   Is the tribunal met: so now you know.   540
'Then I presume those gentlemen with wings,'
   Said Wilkes, 'are cherubs; and that soul below
Looks much like George the Third, but to my mind
A good deal older—Bless me! is he blind?'

LXIX

'He is what you behold him, and his doom
   Depends upon his deeds,' the Angel said;
'If you have aught to arraign in him, the tomb
   Gives licence to the humblest beggar's head
To lift itself against the loftiest.'—'Some,'
   Said Wilkes, 'don't wait to see them laid in lead,   550
For such a liberty—and I, for one,
Have told them what I thought beneath the sun.'

LXX

'*Above* the sun repeat, then, what thou hast
   To urge against him,' said the Archangel. 'Why,'
Replied the spirit, 'since old scores are past,
   Must I turn evidence? In faith, not I.
Besides, I beat him hollow at the last,
   With all his Lords and Commons: in the sky
I don't like ripping up old stories, since
His conduct was but natural in a prince.   560

LXXI

'Foolish, no doubt, and wicked, to oppress
   A poor unlucky devil without a shilling;
But then I blame the man himself much less
   Than Bute and Grafton, and shall be unwilling
To see him punish'd here for their excess,
   Since they were both damn'd long ago, and still in
Their place below: for me, I have forgiven,
And vote his "habeas corpus" into heaven.'

LXXII

'Wilkes,' said the Devil, 'I understand all this;
   You turn'd to half a courtier ere you died,   570
And seem to think it would not be amiss
   To grow a whole one on the other side

124

Of Charon's ferry; you forget that *his*
    Reign is concluded; whatsoe'er betide,
He won't be sovereign more; you've lost your labour,
For at the best he will but be your neighbour.

LXXIII

'However, I knew what to think of it,
    When I beheld you in your jesting way,
Flitting and whispering round about the spit
    Where Belial, upon duty for the day,   580
With Fox's lard was basting William Pitt,
    His pupil; I knew what to think, I say:
That fellow even in hell breeds farther ills;
I'll have him *gagg'd*—'twas one of his own bills.

LXXIV

'Call Junius!' From the crowd a shadow stalk'd,
    And at the name there was a general squeeze,
So that the very ghosts no longer walk'd
    In comfort, at their own aërial ease,
But were all ramm'd, and jamm'd (but to be balk'd,
    As we shall see), and jostled hands and knees,   590
Like wind compress'd and pent within a bladder,
Or like a human colic, which is sadder.

LXXV

The shadow came—a tall, thin, grey-hair'd figure,
    That look'd as it had been a shade on earth;
Quick in its motions, with an air of vigour,
    But nought to mark its breeding or its birth;
Now it wax'd little, then again grew bigger,
    With now an air of gloom, or savage mirth;
But as you gazed upon its features, they
Changed every instant—to *what*, none could say.   600

125

The more intently the ghosts gazed, the less
  Could they distinguish whose the features were;
The Devil himself seem'd puzzled even to guess;
  They varied like a dream—now here, now there;
And several people swore from out the press,
  They knew him perfectly; and one could swear
He was his father: upon which another
Was sure he was his mother's cousin's brother:

Another, that he was a duke, or knight,
  An orator, a lawyer, or a priest,   610
A nabob, a man-midwife; but the wight
  Mysterious changed his countenance at least
As oft as they their minds; though in full sight
  He stood, the puzzle only was increased;
The man was a phantasmagoria in
Himself—he was so volatile and thin.

The moment that you had pronounced him *one*,
  Presto! his face changed, and he was another;
And when that change was hardly well put on,
  It varied, till I don't think his own mother   620
(If that he had a mother) would her son
  Have known, he shifted so from one to t'other;
Till guessing from a pleasure grew a task,
At this epistolary 'Iron Mask.'

For sometimes he like Cerberus would seem—
  'Three gentlemen at once' (as sagely says
Good Mrs. Malaprop); then you might deem
  That he was not even *one*; now many rays

Were flashing round him; and now a thick steam
   Hid him from sight—like fogs on London days: 630
Now Burke, now Tooke, he grew to people's fancies,
And certes often like Sir Philip Francis.

LXXX

I've an hypothesis—'tis quite my own;
   I never let it out till now, for fear
Of doing people harm about the throne,
   And injuring some minister or peer,
On whom the stigma might perhaps be blown;
   It is—my gentle public, lend thine ear!
'Tis, that what Junius we are wont to call
Was *really*, *truly*, nobody at all.   640

LXXXI

I don't see wherefore letters should not be
   Written without hands, since we daily view
Them written without heads; and books, we see,
   Are fill'd as well without the latter too:
And really till we fix on somebody
   For certain sure to claim them as his due,
Their author, like the Niger's mouth, will bother
The world to say if *there* be mouth or author.

LXXXII

'And who and what art thou?' the Archangel said.
   'For *that* you may consult my title-page,'   650
Replied this mighty shadow of a shade:
   'If I have kept my secret half an age,
I scarce shall tell it now.'—'Canst thou upbraid,'
   Continued Michael, 'George Rex, or allege
Aught further?' Junius answer'd, 'You had better
First ask him for *his* answer to my letter:

'My charges upon record will outlast
  The brass of both his epitaph and tomb.'
'Repent'st thou not,' said Michael, 'of some past
  Exaggeration? something which may doom   660
Thyself if false, as him if true? Thou wast
  Too bitter—is it not so?—in thy gloom
Of passion?'—'Passion!' cried the phantom dim,
'I loved my country, and I hated him.

LXXXIV

'What I have written, I have written: let
  The rest be on his head or mine!' So spoke
Old 'Nominis Umbra'; and while speaking yet,
  Away he melted in celestial smoke.
Then Satan said to Michael, 'Don't forget
  To call George Washington, and John Horne Tooke, 670
And Franklin;'—but at this time there was heard
A cry for room, though not a phantom stirr'd.

LXXXV

At length with jostling, elbowing, and the aid
  Of cherubim appointed to that post,
The devil Asmodeus to the circle made
  His way, and look'd as if his journey cost
Some trouble. When his burden down he laid,
  'What's this?' cried Michael; 'why, 'tis not a ghost?'
'I know it,' quoth the incubus; 'but he
Shall be one, if you leave the affair to me.   680

LXXXVI

'Confound the renegado! I have sprain'd
  My left wing, he's so heavy; one would think
Some of his works about his neck were chain'd.
  But to the point; while hovering o'er the brink

128

Of Skiddaw (where as usual it still rain'd),
    I saw a taper, far below me, wink,
And stooping, caught this fellow at a libel—
No less on history than the Holy Bible.

LXXXVII

'The former is the devil's scripture, and
    The latter yours, good Michael: so the affair   690
Belongs to all of us, you understand.
    I snatch'd him up just as you see him there,
And brought him off for sentence out of hand:
    I've scarcely been ten minutes in the air—
At least a quarter it can hardly be:
I dare say that his wife is still at tea.'

LXXXVIII

Here Satan said, 'I know this man of old,
    And have expected him for some time here;
A sillier fellow you will scarce behold,
    Or more conceited in his petty sphere.   700
But surely it was not worth while to fold
    Such trash below your wing, Asmodeus dear:
We had the poor wretch safe (without being bored
With carriage) coming of his own accord.

LXXXIX

But since he's here, let's see what he has done.'
    'Done!' cried Asmodeus, 'he anticipates
The very business you are now upon,
    And scribbles as if head clerk to the Fates.
Who knows to what his ribaldry may run,
    When such an ass as this, like Balaam's, prates?'   710
'Let's hear,' quoth Michael, 'what he has to say:
You know we're bound to that in every way.'

129

Now the bard, glad to get an audience, which
　　By no means often was his case below,
Began to cough, and hawk, and hem, and pitch
　　His voice into that awful note of woe
To all unhappy hearers within reach
　　Of poets when the tide of rhyme's in flow;
But stuck fast with his first hexameter,
Not one of all whose gouty feet would stir.　　　　720

But ere the spavin'd dactyls could be spurr'd
　　Into recitative, in great dismay
Both cherubim and seraphim were heard
　　To murmur loudly through their long array;
And Michael rose ere he could get a word
　　Of all his founder'd verses under way,
And cried, 'For God's sake stop, my friend! 'twere best—
Non Di, non homines—you know the rest.'

A general bustle spread throughout the throng,
　　Which seem'd to hold all verse in detestation;　　730
The angels had of course enough of song
　　When upon service; and the generation
Of ghosts had heard too much in life, not long
　　Before, to profit by a new occasion.
The monarch, mute till then, exclaimed, 'What! what!
Pye come again? No more—no more of that!'

The tumult grew; an universal cough
　　Convulsed the skies, as during a debate,
When Castlereagh has been up long enough
　　(Before he was first minister of state,　　　　740

I mean—the *slaves hear now*); some cried 'Off, off!'
     As at a face; till, grown quite desperate,
The bard Saint Peter pray'd to interpose
(Himself an author) only for his prose.

The varlet was not an ill-favour'd knave;
     A good deal like a vulture in the face,
With a hook nose and a hawk's eye, which gave
     A smart and sharper-looking sort of grace
To his whole aspect, which, though rather grave,
     Was by no means so ugly as his case;   750
But that, indeed, was hopeless as can be,
Quite a poetic felony '*de se.*'

Then Michael blew his trump, and still'd the noise
     With one still greater, as is yet the mode
On earth besides; except some grumbling voice,
     Which now and then will make a slight inroad
Upon decorous silence, few will twice
     Lift up their lungs when fairly overcrow'd;
And now the bard could plead his own bad cause,
With all the attitudes of self-applause.   760

He said—(I only give the heads)—he said,
     He meant no harm in scribbling; 'twas his way
Upon all topics; 'twas, besides, his bread,
     Of which he butter'd both sides; 'twould delay
Too long the assembly (he was pleased to dread),
     And take up rather more time than a day,
To name his works—he would but cite a few—
'Wat Tyler'—'Rhymes on Blenheim'—'Waterloo.'

He had written praises of a regicide;
   He had written praises of all kings whatever;   770
He had written for republics far and wide,
   And then against them bitterer than ever;
For pantisocracy he once had cried
   Aloud, a scheme less normal than 'twas clever;
Then grew a hearty anti-jacobin—
Had turn'd his coat—and would have turn'd his skin.

XCVIII

He had sung against all battles, and again
   In their high praise and glory; he had call'd
Reviewing 'the ungentle craft,' and then
   Become as base a critic as e'er crawl'd—   780
Fed, paid, and pamper'd by the very men
   By whom his muse and morals had been maul'd:
He had written much blank verse, and blanker prose,
And more of both than anybody knows.

XCIX

He had written Wesley's life:—here turning round
   To Satan, 'Sir, I'm ready to write yours,
In two octavo volumes, nicely bound,
   With notes and preface, all that most allures
The pious purchaser; and there's no ground
   For fear, for I can choose my own reviewers: 790
So let me have the proper documents,
That I may add you to my other saints.'

C

Satan bow'd, and was silent. 'Well, if you,
   With amiable modesty, decline
My offer, what says Michael? There are few
   Whose memoirs could be render'd more divine.

Mine is a pen of all work; not so new
    As it was once, but I would make you shine
Like your own trumpet. By the way, my own
Has more of brass in it, and is as well blown.   800

CI

'But talking about trumpets, here's my Vision!
    Now you shall judge, all people; yes, you shall
Judge with my judgment, and by my decision
    Be guided who shall enter heaven or fall.
I settle all these things by intuition,
    Times present, past, to come, heaven, hell, and all,
Like King Alfonso. When I thus see double,
I save the Deity some worlds of trouble.'

CII

He ceased, and drew forth an MS.; and no
    Persuasion on the part of devils, saints,   810
Or angels, now could stop the torrent; so
    He read the first three lines of the contents;
But at the fourth, the whole spiritual show
    Had vanish'd, with variety of scents,
Ambrosial and sulphureous, as they sprang,
Like lightning, off from his 'melodious twang.'

CIII

Those grand heroics acted as a spell:
    The angels stopp'd their ears and plied their pinions;
The devils ran howling, deafen'd, down to hell;
    The ghosts fled, gibbering, for their own dominions— 820
(For 'tis not yet decided where they dwell,
    And I leave every man to his opinions);
Michael took refuge in his trump—but, lo!
His teeth were set on edge, he could not blow!

133

CIV

Saint Peter, who has hitherto been known
  For an impetuous saint, upraised his keys,
And at the fifth line knock'd the poet down;
  Who fell like Phaeton, but more at ease,
Into his lake, for there he did not drown;
  A different web being by the Destinies   830
Woven for the Laureate's final wreath, whene'er
Reform shall happen either here or there.

CV

He first sank to the bottom—like his works,
  But soon rose to the surface—like himself;
For all corrupted things are buoy'd like corks,
  By their own rottenness, light as an elf,
Or wisp that flits o'er a morass: he lurks,
  It may be, still, like dull books on a shelf,
In his own den, to scrawl some 'Life' or 'Vision,'
As Welborn says—'the devil turn'd precisian.'   840

CVI

As for the rest, to come to the conclusion
  Of this true dream, the telescope is gone
Which kept my optics free from all delusion,
  And show'd me what I in my turn have shown;
All I saw farther, in the last confusion,
  Was, that King George slipp'd into heaven for one;
And when the tumult dwindled to a calm,
I left him practising the hundredth psalm.

PART THREE

DON JUAN

Canto the First

'Difficile est propriè communia dicere.'—HORACE.
'Dost thou think, because thou art virtuous, there shall be no more cakes
and ale? Yes, by Saint Anne, and ginger shall be hot i' the mouth, too!'—
SHAKESPEARE, *Twelfth Night, or What You Will.*

Fragment
On the back of the Poet's MS. of Canto I.

I would to heaven that I were so much clay,
   As I am blood, bone, marrow, passion, feeling—
Because at least the past were pass'd away—
   And for the future—(but I write this reeling,
Having got drunk exceedingly to-day,
   So that I seem to stand upon the ceiling)
I say—the future is a serious matter—
And so—for God's sake—hock and sodawater!

Dedication
I

Bob Southey! You're a poet—Poet-laureate,
   And representative of all the race;
Although 'tis true that you turn'd out a Tory at
   Last,—yours has lately been a common case;
And now my Epic Renegade! what are ye at?
   With all the Lakers, in and out of place?
A nest of tuneful persons, to my eye
Like 'four and twenty Blackbirds in a pye;

'Which pye being open'd they began to sing'
   (This old song and new simile holds good),   10
'A dainty dish to set before the King,'
   Or Regent, who admires such kind of food;—
And Coleridge, too, has lately taken wing,
   But like a hawk encumber'd with his hood,—
Explaining metaphysics to the nation—
I wish he would explain his Explanation.

III

You Bob! are rather insolent, you know,
   At being disappointed in your wish
To supersede all warblers here below,
   And be the only Blackbird in the dish;   20
And then you overstrain yourself, or so,
   And tumble downward like the flying fish
Gasping on deck, because you soar too high, Bob,
And fall, for lack of moisture quite a-dry, Bob!

IV

And Wordsworth, in a rather long 'Excursion'
   (I think the quarto holds five hundred pages),
Has given a sample from the vasty version
   Of his new system to perplex the sages;
'Tis poetry—at least by his assertion,
   And may appear so when the dog-star rages—   30
And he who understands it would be able
To add a story to the Tower of Babel.

V

You—Gentlemen! by dint of long seclusion
   From better company, have kept your own
At Keswick, and, through still continued fusion
   Of one another's minds, at last have grown

To deem as a most logical conclusion,
    That Poesy has wreaths for you alone:
There is a narrowness in such a notion,
Which makes me wish you'd change your lakes for ocean.   40

VI

I would not imitate the petty thought,
    Nor coin my self-love to so base a vice,
For all the glory your conversion brought,
    Since gold alone should not have been its price.
You have your salary: was't for that you wrought?
    And Wordsworth has his place in the Excise.
You're shabby fellows—true—but poets still,
And duly seated on the immortal hill.

VII

Your bays may hide the baldness of your brows—
    Perhaps some virtuous blushes;—let them go—   50
To you I envy neither fruit nor boughs—
    And for the fame you would engross below,
The field is universal, and allows
    Scope to all such as feel the inherent glow:
Scott, Rogers, Campbell, Moore, and Crabbe, will try
'Gainst you the question with posterity.

VIII

For me, who, wandering with pedestrian Muses,
    Contend not with you on the winged steed,
I wish your fate may yield ye, when she chooses,
    The fame you envy, and the skill you need;   60
And recollect a poet nothing loses
    In giving to his brethern their full meed
Of merit, and complaint of present days
Is not the certain path to future praise.

IX

He that reserves his laurels for posterity
  (Who does not often claim the bright reversion)
Has generally no great crop to spare it, he
  Being only injured by his own assertion;
And although here and there some glorious rarity
  Arise like Titan from the sea's immersion,   70
The major part of such appellants go
To—God knows where—for no one else can know.

X

If, fallen in evil days on evil tongues,
  Milton appealed to the Avenger, Time,
If Time, the Avenger, execrates his wrongs,
  And makes the word 'Miltonic' mean '*sublime*,'
He deign'd not to belie his soul in songs,
  Nor turn his very talent to a crime;
He did not loathe the Sire to laud the Son,
But closed the tyrant-hater he begun.   80

XI

Think'st thou, could he—the blind Old Man—arise,
  Like Samuel from the grave, to freeze once more
The blood of monarchs with his prophecies,
  Or be alive again—again all hoar
With time and trials, and those helpless eyes,
  And heartless daughters—worn—and pale—and poor;
Would *he* adore a sultan? *he* obey
The intellectual eunuch Castlereagh?

XII

Cold-blooded, smooth-faced, placid miscreant!
  Dabbling its sleek young hands in Erin's gore,   90
And thus for wider carnage taught to pant,
  Transferr'd to gorge upon a sister shore,

138

The vulgarest tool that Tyranny could want,
  With just enough of talent, and no more,
To lengthen fetters by another fix'd,
And offer poison long already mix'd.

XIII

An orator of such set trash of phrase
  Ineffably—legitimately vile,
That even its grossest flatterers dare not praise,
  Nor foes—all nations—condescend to smile;   100
Not even a sprightly blunder's spark can blaze
  From that Ixion grindstone's ceaseless toil,
That turns and turns to give the world a notion
Of endless torments and perpetual motion.

XIV

A bungler even in its disgusting trade,
  And botching, patching, leaving still behind
Something of which its masters are afraid,
  States to be curb'd, and thoughts to be confined,
Conspiracy or Congress to be made—
  Cobbling at manacles for all mankind—   110
A tinkering slave-maker, who mends old chains,
With God and man's abhorrence for its gains.

XV

If we may judge of matter by the mind,
  Emasculated to the marrow *It*
Hath but two objects, how to serve, and bind,
  Deeming the chain it wears even men may fit,
Eutropius of its many masters,—blind
  To worth as freedom, wisdom as to wit,
Fearless—because *no* feeling dwells in ice,
Its very courage stagnates to a vice.   120

139

XVI

Where shall I turn me not to *view* its bonds,
　For I will never *feel* them;—Italy!
Thy late reviving Roman soul desponds
　Beneath the lie this State-thing breathed o'er thee—
Thy clanking chain, and Erin's yet green wounds,
　Have voices—tongues to cry aloud for me.
Europe has slaves, allies, kings, armies still,
And Southey lives to sing them very ill.

XVII

Meantime, Sir Laureate, I proceed to dedicate,
　In honest simple verse, this song to you.　　　　130
And, if in flattering strains I do not predicate,
　'Tis that I still retain my 'buff and blue;'
My politics as yet are all to educate:
　Apostasy's so fashionable, too,
To keep *one* creed's a task grown quite Herculean:
Is it not so, my Tory, ultra-Julian?

VENICE, *September* 16, 1818.

Canto the First

I

I want a hero: an uncommon want,
　When every year and month sends forth a new one,
Till, after cloying the gazettes with cant,
　The age discovers he is not the true one:
Of such as these I should not care to vaunt,
　I'll therefore take our ancient friend Don Juan—
We all have seen him, in the pantomime,
Sent to the devil somewhat ere his time.

II

Vernon, the butcher Cumberland, Wolfe, Hawke,
　Prince Ferdinand, Granby, Burgoyne. Keppel, Howe.　　10

Evil and good, have had their tithe of talk,
    And fill'd their sign-posts then, like Wellesley now;
Each in their turn like Banquo's monarchs stalk,
    Followers of fame, 'nine farrow' of that sow:
France, too, had Buonaparté and Dumourier
Recorded in the Moniteur and Courier.

III

Barnave, Brissot, Condorcet, Mirabeau,
    Pétion, Clootz, Danton, Marat, La Fayette,
Were French, and famous people, as we know;
    And there were others, scarce forgotten yet,   20
Joubert, Hoche, Marceau, Lannes, Desaix, Moreau,
    With many of the military set,
Exceedingly remarkable at times,
But not at all adapted to my rhymes.

IV

Nelson was once Britannia's god of war,
    And still should be so, but the tide is turn'd;
There's no more to be said of Trafalgar,
    'Tis with our hero quietly inurn'd;
Because the army's grown more popular,
    At which the naval people are concern'd,   30
Besides, the prince is all for the land-service,
Forgetting Duncan, Nelson, Howe, and Jervis.

V

Brave men were living before Agamemnon
    And since, exceeding valorous and sage,
A good deal like him too, though quite the same none;
    But then they shone not on the poet's page,
And so have been forgotten:—I condemn none,
    But can't find any in the present age
Fit for my poem (that is, for my new one);
So, as I said, I'll take my friend Don Juan.   40

Most epic poets plunge '*in medias res*'
   (Horace makes this the heroic turnpike road),
And then your hero tells, whene'er you please,
   What went before—by way of episode,
While seated after dinner at his ease,
   Beside his mistress in some soft abode,
Palace, or garden, paradise, or cavern,
Which serves the happy couple for a tavern.

VII

That is the usual method, but not mine—
   My way is to begin with the beginning;   50
The regularity of my design
   Forbids all wandering as the worst of sinning,
And therefore I shall open with a line
   (Although it cost me half an hour in spinning)
Narrating somewhat of Don Juan's father,
And also of his mother, if you'd rather.

In Seville was he born, a pleasant city,
   Famous for oranges and women—he
Who has not seen it will be much to pity,
   So says the proverb—and I quite agree;   60
Of all the Spanish towns is none more pretty,
   Cadiz, perhaps—but that you soon may see:—
Don Juan's parents lived beside the river,
A noble stream, and call'd the Guadalquivir.

IX

His father's name was José—*Don*, of course,
   A true Hidalgo, free from every stain
Of Moor or Hebrew blood, he traced his source
   Through the most Gothic gentlemen of Spain;

A better cavalier ne'er mounted horse,
   Or, being mounted, e'er got down again.   70
Than José, who begot our hero, who
Begot—but that's to come——Well, to renew:

X
His mother was a learned lady, famed
   For every branch of every science known—
In every Christian language ever named,
   With virtues equall'd by her wit alone:
She made the cleverest people quite ashamed,
   And even the good with inward envy groan,
Finding themselves so very much exceeded
In their own way by all the things that she did.   80

XI
Her memory was a mine: she knew by heart
   All Calderon and greater part of Lopé,
So that if any actor miss'd his part
   She could have served him for the prompter's copy;
For her Feinagle's were an useless art,
   And he himself obliged to shut up shop—he
Could never make a memory so fine as
That which adorn'd the brain of Donna Inez.

XII
Her favourite science was the mathematical,
   Her noblest virtue was her magnanimity;   90
Her wit (she sometimes tried at wit) was Attic all,
   Her serious sayings darken'd to sublimity;
In short, in all things she was fairly what I call
   A prodigy—her morning dress was dimity,
Her evening silk, or, in the summer, muslin,
And other stuffs, with which I won't stay puzzling.

143

XIII

She knew the Latin—that is, 'the Lord's prayer,'
　　And Greek—the alphabet—I'm nearly sure;
She read some French romances here and there,
　　Although her mode of speaking was not pure;　　　100
For native Spanish she had no great care,
　　At least her conversation was obscure;
Her thoughts were theorems, her words a problem,
As if she deem'd that mystery would ennoble 'em.

She liked the English and the Hebrew tongue,
　　And said there was analogy between 'em;
She proved it somehow out of sacred song,
　　But I must leave the proofs to those who've seen 'em,
But this I heard her say, and can't be wrong,
　　And all may think which way their judgments lean 'em,　110
' 'Tis strange—the Hebrew noun which means "I am,"
The English always use to govern d—n.'

XV

Some women use their tongues—she *look'd* a lecture,
　　Each eye a sermon, and her brow a homily,
An all-in-all sufficient self-director,
　　Like the lamented late Sir Samuel Romilly,
The Law's expounder, and the State's corrector,
　　Whose suicide was almost an anomaly—
One sad example more, that 'All is vanity,'—
(The jury brought their verdict in 'Insanity.')　　　120

In short, she was a walking calculation,
　　Miss Edgeworth's novels stepping from their covers,
Or Mrs. Trimmer's books on education,
　　Or 'Cœlebs' Wife' set out in quest of lovers,

Morality's prim personification,
    In which not Envy's self a flaw discovers;
To others' share let 'female errors fall,'
For she had not even one—the worst of all.

XVII

Oh! she was perfect past all parallel—
    Of any modern female saint's comparison;   130
So far above the cunning powers of hell,
    Her guardian angel had given up his garrison;
Even her minutest motions went as well
    As those of the best time-piece made by Harrison:
In virtues nothing earthly could surpass her,
Save thine 'incomparable oil,' Macassar!

XVIII

Perfect she was, but as perfection is
    Insipid in this naughty world of ours,
Where our first parents never learn'd to kiss
    Till they were exiled from their earlier bowers,   140
Where all was peace, and innocence, and bliss
    (I wonder how they got through the twelve hours),
Don José, like a lineal son of Eve,
Went plucking various fruit without her leave.

XIX

He was a mortal of the careless kind,
    With no great love for learning, or the learn'd,
Who chose to go where'er he had a mind,
    And never dream'd his lady was concern'd;
The world, as usual, wickedly inclined
    To see a kingdom or a house o'erturn'd,   150
Whisper'd he had a mistress, some said *two*,
But for domestic quarrels *one* will do.

XX

Now Donna Inez had, with all her merit,
    A great opinion of her own good qualities;
Neglect, indeed, requires a saint to bear it,
    And such, indeed, she was in her moralities;
But then she had a devil of a spirit,
    And sometimes mix'd up fancies with realities,
And let few opportunities escape
Of getting her liege lord into a scrape.   160

XXI

This was an easy matter with a man
    Oft in the wrong, and never on his guard;
And even the wisest, do the best they can,
    Have moments, hours, and days, so unprepared,
That you might 'brain them with their lady's fan';
    And sometimes ladies hit exceeding hard,
And fans turn into falchions in fair hands,
And why and wherefore no one understands.

XXII

'Tis pity learned virgins ever wed
    With persons of no sort of education,   170
Or gentlemen, who, though well born and bred,
    Grow tired of scientific conversation;
I don't choose to say much upon this head,
    I'm a plain man, and in a single station,
But—Oh! ye lords of ladies intellectual,
Inform us truly have they not hen-peck'd you all?

XXIII

Don José and his lady quarrell'd—*why*,
    Not any of the many could divine,
Though several thousand people chose to try,
    'Twas surely no concern of theirs nor mine;   180

146

I loathe that low vice—curiosity;
    But if there's anything in which I shine,
'Tis in arranging all my friends' affairs,
Not having, of my own, domestic cares.

XXIV

And so I interfered, and with the best
    Intentions, but their treatment was not kind;
I think the foolish people were possess'd,
    For neither of them could I ever find,
Although their porter afterwards confess'd—
    But that's no matter, and the worst's behind,   190
For little Juan o'er me threw, down stairs,
A pail of housemaid's water unawares.

XXV

A little curly-headed, good-for-nothing,
    And mischief-making monkey from his birth;
His parents ne'er agreed except in doting
    Upon the most unquiet imp on earth;
Instead of quarrelling, had they been but both in
    Their senses, they'd have sent young master forth
To school, or had him soundly whipp'd at home,
To teach him manners for the time to come.   200

XXVI

Don José and the Donna Inez led
    For some time an unhappy sort of life,
Wishing each other, not divorced, but dead;
    They lived respectably as man and wife,
Their conduct was exceedingly well-bred,
    And gave no outward signs of inward strife,
Until at length the smother'd fire broke out,
And put the business past all kind of doubt.

XXVII

For Inez call'd some druggists and physicians,
    And tried to prove her loving lord was *mad*,   210
But as he had some lucid intermissions,
    She next decided he was only *bad*;
Yet when they ask'd her for her depositions,
    No sort of explanation could be had,
Save that her duty both to man and God
Required this conduct—which seem'd very odd.

XXVIII

She kept a journal, where his faults were noted,
    And open'd certain trunks of books and letters,
All of which might, if occasion served, be quoted;
    And then she had all Seville for abettors,   220
Besides her good old grandmother (who doted);
    The hearers of her case became repeaters,
Then advocates, inquisitors, and judges,
Some for amusement, others for old grudges.

XXIX

And then this best and meekest woman bore
    With such serenity her husband's woes,
Just as the Spartan ladies did of yore,
    Who saw their spouses kill'd, and nobly chose
Never to say a word about them more—
    Calmly she heard each calumny that rose,   230
And saw *his* agonies with such sublimity,
That all the world exclaim'd, 'What magnanimity!'

XXX

No doubt this patience, when the world is damning us,
    Is philosophic in our former friends;
'Tis also pleasant to be deem'd magnanimous,
    The more so in obtaining our own ends;

And what the lawyers call a '*malus animus*'
    Conduct like this by no means comprehends:
Revenge in person's certainly no virtue,
But then 'tis not *my* fault, if *others* hurt you.   240

XXXI

And if our quarrels should rip up old stories,
    And help them with a lie or two additional,
I'm not to blame, as you well know—no more is
    Any one else—they were become traditional;
Besides, their resurrection aids our glories
    By contrast, which is what we just were wishing all:
And science profits by this resurrection—
Dead scandals form good subjects for dissection.

XXXII

Their friends had tried at reconciliation,
    Then their relations, who made matters worse,   250
('Twere hard to tell upon a like occasion
    To whom it may be best to have recourse—
I can't say much for friend or yet relation):
    The lawyers did their utmost for divorce,
But scarce a fee was paid on either side
Before, unluckily, Don José died.

XXXIII

He died: and most unluckily, because,
    According to all hints I could collect
From counsel learned in those kinds of laws
    (Although their talk's obscure and circumspect),   260
His death contrived to spoil a charming cause;
    A thousand pities also with respect
To public feeling, which on this occasion
Was manifested in a great sensation.

XXXIV

But ah! he died; and buried with him lay
   The public feeling and the lawyers' fees:
His house was sold, his servants sent away,
   A Jew took one of his two mistresses,
A priest the other—at least so they say:
   I ask'd the doctors after his disease—   270
He died of the slow fever called the tertian,
And left his widow to her own aversion.

Yet José was an honourable man,
   That I must say, who knew him very well;
Therefore his frailties I'll no further scan,
   Indeed there were not many more to tell:
And if his passions now and then outran
   Discretion, and were not so peaceable
As Numa's (who was also named Pompilius),
He had been ill brought up, and was born bilious.   280

XXXVI

Whate'er might be his worthlessness or worth,
   Poor fellow! he had many things to wound him,
Let's own—since it can do no good on earth—
   It was a trying moment that which found him
Standing alone beside his desolate hearth,
   Where all his household gods lay shiver'd round him:
No choice was left his feelings or his pride,
Save death or Doctors' Commons—so he died.

Dying intestate, Juan was sole heir
   To a chancery suit, and messuages and lands,   290
Which, with a long minority and care,
   Promised to turn out well in proper hands:

Inez became sole guardian, which was fair,
    And answer'd but to nature's just demands;
An only son left with an only mother
Is brought up much more wisely than another.

XXXVIII

Sagest of women, even of widows, she
    Resolved that Juan should be quite a paragon,
And worthy of the noblest pedigree:
    (His sire was of Castile, his dam from Aragon).   300
Then for accomplishments of chivalry,
    In case our lord the king should go to war again,
He learn'd the arts of riding, fencing, gunnery,
And how to scale a fortress—or a nunnery.

XXXIX

But that which Donna Inez most desired,
    And saw into herself each day before all
The learned tutors whom for him she hired,
    Was, that his breeding should be strictly moral:
Much into all his studies she inquired,
    And so they were submitted first to her all,   310
Arts, sciences, no branch was made a mystery
To Juan's eyes, excepting natural history.

XL

The languages, especially the dead,
    The sciences, and most of all the abstruse,
The arts, at least all such as could be said
    To be the most remote from common use,
In all these he was much and deeply read:
    But not a page of anything that's loose,
Or hints continuation of the species,
Was ever suffer'd, lest he should grow vicious.   320

XLI

His classic studies made a little puzzle,
  Because of filthy loves of gods and goddesses,
Who in the earlier ages raised a bustle,
  But never put on pantaloons or bodices;
His reverend tutors had at times a tussle,
  And for their Æneids, Iliads, and Odysseys,
Were forced to make an odd sort of apology,
For Donna Inez dreaded the Mythology.

Ovid's a rake, as half his verses show him,
  Anacreon's morals are a still worse sample,   330
Catullus scarcely has a decent poem,
  I don't think Sappho's Ode a good example,
Although Longinus tells us there is no hymn
  Where the sublime soars forth on wings more ample;
But Virgil's songs are pure, except that horrid one
Beginning with 'Formosum Pastor Corydon.'

XLIII

Lucretius' irreligion is too strong
  For early stomachs, to prove wholesome food;
I can't help thinking Juvenal was wrong,
  Although no doubt his real intent was good,   340
For speaking out so plainly in his song,
  So much indeed as to be downright rude;
And then what proper person can be partial
To all those nauseous epigrams of Martial?

Juan was taught from out the best edition,
  Expurgated by learned men, who place,
Judiciously, from out the schoolboy's vision,
  The grosser parts; but, fearful to deface

Too much their modest bard by this omission,
  And pitying sore this mutilated case,   350
They only add them all in an appendix,
  Which saves, in fact, the trouble of an index;

XLV

For there we have them all 'at one fell swoop,'
  Instead of being scatter'd through the pages;
They stand forth marshall'd in a handsome troop,
  To meet the ingenuous youth of future ages,
Till some less rigid editor shall stoop
  To call them back into their separate cages,
Instead of standing staring all together,
Like garden gods—and not so decent either.   360

XLVI

The Missal too (it was the family Missal)
  Was ornamented in a sort of way
Which ancient mass-books often are, and this all
  Kinds of grotesques illumined; and how they,
Who saw those figures on the margin kiss all,
  Could turn their optics to the text and pray,
Is more than I know—But Don Juan's mother
Kept this herself, and gave her son another.

XLVII

Sermons he read, and lectures he endured,
  And homilies, and lives of all the saints;   370
To Jerome and to Chrysostom inured,
  He did not take such studies for restraints;
But how faith is acquired, and then insured,
  So well not one of the aforesaid paints
As Saint Augustine in his fine Confessions,
Which make the reader envy his transgressions.

XLVIII

This, too, was a seal'd book to little Juan—
  I can't but say that his mamma was right,
If such an education was the true one.
  She scarcely trusted him from out her sight;   380
Her maids were old, and if she took a new one,
  You might be sure she was a perfect fright,
She did this during even her husband's life—
I recommend as much to every wife.

Young Juan wax'd in godliness and grace;
  At six a charming child, and at eleven
With all the promise of as fine a face
  As e'er to man's maturer growth was given.
He studied steadily and grew apace,
  And seem'd, at least, in the right road to heaven,   390
For half his days were pass'd at church, the other
Between his tutors, confessor, and mother.

L

At six, I said, he was a charming child,
  At twelve he was a fine, but quiet boy;
Although in infancy a little wild,
  They tamed him down amongst them; to destroy
His natural spirit not in vain they toil'd,
  At least it seem'd so; and his mother's joy
Was to declare how sage, and still, and steady,
Her young philosopher was grown already.   400

I had my doubts, perhaps I have them still,
  But what I say is neither here nor there
knew his father well, and have some skill
  In character—but it would not be fair

From sire to son to augur good or ill:
    He and his wife were an ill sorted pair—
But scandal's my aversion—I protest
Against all evil speaking, even in jest.

LII

For my part I say nothing—nothing—but
    This I will say—my reasons are my own—   410
That if I had an only son to put
    To school (as God be praised that I have none),
'Tis not with Donna Inez I would shut
    Him up to learn his catechism alone,
No—no—I'd send him out betimes to college,
For there it was I pick'd up my own knowledge.

LIII

For there one learns—'tis not for me to boast,
    Though I acquired—but I pass over *that*,
As well as all the Greek I since have lost:
    I say that there's the place—but '*Verbum sat*,'   420
I think I pick'd up too, as well as most,
    Knowledge of matters—but no matter *what*—
I never married—but, I think, I know
That sons should not be educated so.

LIV

Young Juan now was sixteen years of age,
    Tall, handsome, slender, but well knit: he seem'd
Active, though not so sprightly, as a page;
    And everybody but his mother deem'd
Him almost man; but she flew in a rage
    And bit her lips (for else she might have scream'd)   430
If any said so, for to be precocious
Was in her eyes a thing the most atrocious.

LV

Amongst her numerous acquaintance, all
    Selected for discretion and devotion,
There was the Donna Julia, whom to call
    Pretty were but to give a feeble notion
Of many charms in her as natural
    As sweetness to the flower, or salt to ocean,
Her zone to Venus, or his bow to Cupid
(But this last simile is trite and stupid).   440

The darkness of her Oriental eye
    Accorded with her Moorish origin;
(Her blood was not all Spanish, by the by;
    In Spain, you know, this is a sort of sin).
When proud Granada fell, and, forced to fly,
    Boabdil wept, of Donna Julia's kin
Some went to Africa, some stay'd in Spain,
Her great great grandmamma chose to remain.

LVII

She married (I forget the pedigree)
    With an Hidalgo, who transmitted down   450
His blood less noble than such blood should be;
    At such alliances his sires would frown,
In that point so precise in each degree
    That they bred *in and in*, as might be shown,
Marrying their cousins—nay, their aunts, and nieces,
Which always spoils the breed, if it increases.

This heathenish cross restored the breed again,
    Ruin'd its blood, but much improved its flesh;
For from a root the ugliest in old Spain
    Sprung up a branch as beautiful as fresh;   460

The sons no more were short, the daughters plain:
  But there's a rumour which I fain would hush,
'Tis said that Donna Julia's grandmamma
Produced her Don more heirs at love than law.

LIX

However this might be, the race went on
  Improving still through every generation,
Until it centred in an only son,
  Who left an only daughter: my narration
May have suggested that this single one
  Could be but Julia (whom on this occasion   470
I shall have much to speak about), and she
Was married, charming, chaste, and twenty-three.

LX

Her eye (I'm very fond of handsome eyes)
  Was large and dark, suppressing half its fire
Until she spoke, then through its soft disguise
  Flash'd an expression more of pride than ire,
And love than either; and there would arise
  A something in them which was not desire,
But would have been, perhaps, but for the soul
Which struggled through and chasten'd down the whole.   480

LXI

Her glossy hair was cluster'd o'er a brow
  Bright with intelligence, and fair, and smooth;
Her eyebrow's shape was like the aërial bow,
  Her cheek all purple with the beam of youth,
Mounting, at times, to a transparent glow,
  As if her veins ran lightning; she, in sooth,
Possess'd an air and grace by no means common:
Her stature tall—I hate a dumpy woman.

LXII

Wedded she was some years, and to a man
   Of fifty, and such husbands are in plenty;   490
And yet, I think, instead of such a ONE
   'Twere better to have TWO of five-and-twenty,
Especially in countries near the sun:
   And now I think on't, 'mi vien in mente,'
Ladies even of the most uneasy virtue
Prefer a spouse whose age is short of thirty.

LXIII

'Tis a sad thing, I cannot choose but say,
   And all the fault of that indecent sun,
Who cannot leave alone our helpless clay,
   But will keep baking, broiling, burning on,   500
That howsoever people fast and pray,
   The flesh is frail, and so the soul undone:
What men call gallantry, and gods adultery,
Is much more common where the climate's sultry.

LXIV

Happy the nations of the moral North!
   Where all is virtue, and the winter season
Sends sin, without a rag on, shivering forth
   ('Twas snow that brought St. Anthony to reason);
Where juries cast up what a wife is worth,
   By laying whate'er sum, in mulct, they please on   510
The lover, who must pay a handsome price,
Because it is a marketable vice.

LXV

Alfonso was the name of Julia's lord,
   A man well looking for his years, and who
Was neither much beloved nor yet abhorr'd:
   They lived together as most people do,

Suffering each other's foibles by accord,
    And not exactly either *one* or *two;*
Yet he was jealous, though he did not show it,
For jealousy dislikes the world to know it.   520

LXVI

Julia was—yet I never could see why—
    With Donna Inez quite a favourite friend;
Between their tastes there was small sympathy,
    For not a line had Julia ever penn'd:
Some people whisper (but, no doubt, they lie,
    For malice still imputes some private end)
That Inez had, ere Don Alfonso's marriage,
Forgot with him her very prudent carriage;

LXVII

And that still keeping up the old connexion,
    Which time had lately render'd much more chaste,   530
She took his lady also in affection,
    And certainly this course was much the best:
She flatter'd Julia with her sage protection,
    And complimented Don Alfonso's taste;
And if she could not (who can?) silence scandal,
At least she left it a more slender handle.

LXVIII

I can't tell whether Julia saw the affair
    With other people's eyes, or if her own
Discoveries made, but none could be aware
    Of this, at least no symptom e'er was shown;   540
Perhaps she did not know, or did not care,
    Indifferent from the first, or callous grown:
I'm really puzzled what to think or say,
She kept her counsel in so close a way.

LXIX

Juan she saw, and, as a pretty child,
   Caress'd him often—such a thing might be
Quite innocently done, and harmless styled,
   When she had twenty years, and thirteen he;
But I am not so sure I should have smiled
   When he was sixteen, Julia twenty-three;   550
These few short years make wondrous alterations,
Particularly amongst sun-burnt nations.

Whate'er the cause might be, they had become
   Changed; for the dame grew distant, the youth shy,
Their looks cast down, their greetings almost dumb,
   And much embarrassment in either eye;
There surely will be little doubt with some
   That Donna Julia knew the reason why,
But as for Juan, he had no more notion
Than he who never saw the sea of ocean.   560

LXXI

Yet Julia's very coldness still was kind,
   And tremulously gentle her small hand
Withdrew itself from his, but left behind
   A little pressure, thrilling, and so bland
And slight, so very slight, that to the mind
   'Twas but a doubt; but ne'er magician's wand
Wrought change with all Armida's fairy art
Like what this light touch left on Juan's heart.

And if she met him, though she smiled no more,
   She look'd a sadness sweeter than her smile,   570
As if her heart had deeper thoughts in store
   She must not own, but cherish'd more the while

For that compression in its burning core;
　Even innocence itself has many a wile,
And will not dare to trust itself with truth,
And love is taught hypocrisy from youth.

LXXIII

But passion most dissembles, yet betrays
　Even by its darkness; as the blackest sky
Foretells the heaviest tempest, it displays
　Its workings through the vainly guarded eye,　　580
And in whatever aspect it arrays
　Itself, 'tis still the same hypocrisy:
Coldness or anger, even disdain or hate,
Are masks it often wears, and still too late.

LXXIV

Then there were sighs, the deeper for suppression,
　And stolen glances, sweeter for the theft,
And burning blushes, though for no transgression,
　Tremblings when met, and restlessness when left;
All these are little preludes to possession,
　Of which young passion cannot be bereft,　　590
And merely tend to show how greatly love is
Embarrass'd at first starting with a novice.

LXXV

Poor Julia's heart was in an awkward state;
　She felt it going, and resolved to make
The noblest efforts for herself and mate,
　For honour's, pride's, religion's, virtue's sake.
Her resolutions were most truly great,
　And almost might have made a Tarquin quake:
She pray'd the Virgin Mary for her grace,
As being the best judge of a lady's case.　　600

LXXVI

She vow'd she never would see Juan more,
  And next day paid a visit to his mother,
And look'd extremely at the opening door,
  Which, by the Virgin's grace, let in another;
Grateful she was, and yet a little sore—
  Again it opens, it can be no other,
'Tis surely Juan now—No! I'm afraid
That night the Virgin was no further pray'd.

LXXVII

She now determined that a virtuous woman
  Should rather face and overcome temptation,   610
That flight was base and dastardly, and no man
  Should ever give her heart the least sensation;
That is to say, a thought beyond the common
  Preference, that we must feel upon occasion,
For people who are pleasanter than others,
But then they only seem so many brothers.

LXXVIII

And even if by chance—and who can tell?
  The devil's so very sly—she should discover
That all within was not so very well,
  And, if still free, that such or such a lover   620
Might please perhaps, a virtuous wife can quell
  Such thoughts, and be the better when they're over;
And if the man should ask, 'tis but denial:
I recommend young ladies to make trial.

LXXIX

And then there are such things as love divine,
  Bright and immaculate, unmix'd and pure,
Such as the angels think so very fine,
  And matrons, who would be no less secure,

Platonic, perfect, 'just such love as mine':
    Thus Julia said—and thought so, to be sure;   630
And so I'd have her think, were I the man
On whom her reveries celestial ran.

LXXX

Such love is innocent, and may exist
    Between young persons without any danger:
A hand may first, and then a lip be kist;
    For my part, to such doings I'm a stranger,
But *hear* these freedoms form the utmost list
    Of all o'er which such love may be a ranger:
If people go beyond, 'tis quite a crime,
But not my fault—I tell them all in time.   640

LXXXI

Love, then, but love within its proper limits
    Was Julia's innocent determination
In young Don Juan's favour, and to him its
    Exertion might be useful on occasion;
And, lighted at too pure a shrine to dim its
    Ethereal lustre, with what sweet persuasion
He might be taught, by love and her together—
I really don't know what, nor Julia either.

LXXXII

Fraught with this fine intention, and well fenced
    In mail of proof—her purity of soul,   650
She, for the future of her strength convinced,
    And that her honour was a rock, or mole,
Exceeding sagely from that hour dispensed
    With any kind of troublesome control;
But whether Julia to the task was equal
Is that which must be mention'd in the sequel.

LXXXIII

Her plan she deem'd both innocent and feasible,
   And, surely, with a stripling of sixteen
Not scandal's fangs could fix on much that's seizable,
   Or if they did so, satisfied to mean   660
Nothing but what was good, her breast was peaceable:
   A quiet conscience makes one so serene!
Christians have burnt each other, quite persuaded
That all the Apostles would have done as they did.

LXXXIV

And if in the mean time her husband died,
   But Heaven forbid that such a thought should cross
Her brain, though in a dream! (and then she sigh'd)
   Never could she survive that common loss;
But just suppose that moment should betide,
   I only say suppose it—*inter nos.*   670
(This should be *entre nous,* for Julia thought
In French, but then the rhyme would go for nought.)

LXXXV

I only say, suppose this supposition:
   Juan being then grown up to man's estate
Would fully suit a widow of condition,
   Even seven years hence it would not be too late;
And in the interim (to pursue this vision)
   The mischief, after all, could not be great,
For he would learn the rudiments of love,
I mean the seraph way of those above.   680

LXXXVI

So much for Julia. Now we'll turn to Juan.
   Poor little fellow! He had no idea
Of his own case, and never hit the true one;
   In feelings quick as Ovid's Miss Medea,

He puzzled over what he found a new one.
    But not as yet imagined it could be a
Thing quite in course, and not at all alarming,
Which, with a little patience, might grow charming.

LXXXVII

Silent and pensive, idle, restless, slow,
    His home deserted for the lonely wood,   690
Tormented with a wound he could not know,
    His, like all deep grief, plunged in solitude:
I'm fond myself of solitude or so,
    But then, I beg it may be understood,
By solitude I mean a Sultan's, not
A hermit's, with a harem for a grot.

LXXXVIII

'Oh Love! in such a wilderness as this,
    Where transport and security entwine,
Here is the empire of thy perfect bliss,
    And here thou art a god indeed divine.'   700
The bard I quote from does not sing amiss,
    With the exception of the second line,
For that same twining 'transport and security'
Are twisted to a phrase of some obscurity.

LXXXIX

The poet meant, no doubt, and thus appeals
    To the good sense and senses of mankind,
The very thing which everybody feels,
    As all have found on trial, or may find,
That no one likes to be disturb'd at meals
    Or love.—I won't say more about 'entwined'   710
Or 'transport,' as we knew all that before,
But beg 'Security' will bolt the door.

165

XC

Young Juan wander'd by the glassy brooks,
   Thinking unutterable things; he threw
Himself at length within the leafy nooks
   Where the wild branch of the cork forest grew;
There poets find materials for their books,
   And every now and then we read them through,
So that their plan and prosody are eligible,
Unless, like Wordsworth, they prove unintelligible.   720

XCI

He, Juan (and not Wordsworth), so pursued
   His self-communion with his own high soul,
Until his mighty heart, in its great mood,
   Had mitigated part, though not the whole
Of its disease; he did the best he could
   With things not very subject to control,
And turn'd, without perceiving his condition,
Like Coleridge, into a metaphysician.

XCII

He thought about himself, and the whole earth,
   Of man the wonderful, and of the stars,   730
And how the deuce they ever could have birth;
   And then he thought of earthquakes, and of wars,
How many miles the moon might have in girth,
   Of air-balloons, and of the many bars
To perfect knowledge of the boundless skies;—
And then he thought of Donna Julia's eyes.

XCIII

In thoughts like these true wisdom may discern
   Longings sublime, and aspirations high,
Which some are born with, but the most part learn
   To plague themselves withal, they know not why: 740

'Twas strange that one so young should thus concern
    His brain about the action of the sky;
If *you* think 'twas philosophy that this did,
I can't help thinking puberty assisted.

XCIV

He pored upon the leaves, and on the flowers,
    And heard a voice in all the winds; and then
He thought of wood-nymphs and immortal bowers,
    And how the goddesses came down to men:
He miss'd the pathway, he forgot the hours,
    And when he look'd upon his watch again,   750
He found how much old Time had been a winner—
He also found that he had lost his dinner.

XCV

Sometimes he turn'd to gaze upon his book,
    Boscan or Garcillasso;—by the wind
Even as the page is rustled while we look,
    So by the poesy of his own mind
Over the mystic leaf his soul was shook,
    As if 'twere one whereon magicians bind
Their spells, and give them to the passing gale
According to some good old woman's tale.   760

XCVI

Thus would he while his lonely hours away
    Dissatisfied, not knowing what he wanted;
Nor glowing reverie, nor poet's lay,
    Could yield his spirit that for which it panted,
A bosom, whereon he his head might lay,
    And hear the heart beat with the love it granted,
With——several other things, which I forget,
Or which, at least, I need not mention yet.

XCVII

Those lonely walks, and lengthening reveries,
  Could not escape the gentle Julia's eyes;   770
She saw that Juan was not at his ease;
  But that which chiefly may, and must surprise,
Is, that the Donna Inez did not tease
  Her only son with question or surmise;
Whether it was she did not see, or would not,
Or, like all very clever people, could not.

XCVIII

This may seem strange, but yet 'tis very common;
  For instance—gentlemen, whose ladies take
Leave to o'erstep the written rights of woman,
  And break the——Which commandment is't they break? 780
(I have forgot the number, and think no man
  Should rashly quote, for fear of a mistake.)
I say, when these same gentlemen are jealous,
They make some blunder, which their ladies tell us.

XCIX

A real husband always is suspicious,
  But still no less suspects in the wrong place,
Jealous of some one who had no such wishes,
  Or pandering blindly to his own disgrace,
By harbouring some dear friend extremely vicious;
  The last indeed's infallibly the case: 790
And when the spouse and friend are gone off wholly,
He wonders at their vice, and not his folly.

C

Thus parents also are at times short-sighted;
  Though watchful as the lynx, they ne'er discover,
The while the wicked world beholds delighted,
  Young Hopeful's mistress, or Miss Fanny's lover,

168

Till some confounded escapade has blighted
   The plan of twenty years, and all is over;
And then the mother cries, the father swears,
And wonders why the devil he got heirs.   800

CI

But Inez was so anxious, and so clear
   Of sight, that I must think, on this occasion,
She had some other motive much more near
   For leaving Juan to this new temptation,
But what that motive was, I shan't say here;
   Perhaps to finish Juan's education,
Perhaps to open Don Alfonso's eyes,
In case he thought his wife too great a prize.

CII

It was upon a day, a summer's day;—
   Summer's indeed a very dangerous season,   810
And so is spring about the end of May;
   The sun, no doubt, is the prevailing reason;
But whatsoe'er the cause is, one may say,
   And stand convicted of more truth than treason,
That there are months which nature grows more merry in,—
March has its hares, and May must have its heroine.

CIII

'Twas on a summer's day—the sixth of June:—
   I like to be particular in dates,
Not only of the age, and year, but moon;
   They are a sort of post-house, where the Fates   820
Change horses, making history change its tune,
   Then spur away o'er empires and o'er states,
Leaving at last not much beside chronology,
Excepting the post-obits of theology.

'Twas on the sixth of June, about the hour
    Of half-past six—perhaps still nearer seven—
When Julia sate within as pretty a bower
    As e'er held houri in that heathenish heaven
Described by Mahomet, and Anacreon Moore,
    To whom the lyre and laurels have been given,   830
With all the trophies of triumphant song—
He won them well, and may he wear them long!

She sate, but not alone; I know not well
    How this same interview had taken place,
And even if I knew, I should not tell—
    People should hold their tongues in any case;
No matter how or why the thing befell,
    But there were she and Juan, face to face—
When two such faces are so, 'twould be wise,
But very difficult, to shut their eyes.   840

How beautiful she look'd! her conscious heart
    Glow'd in her cheek, and yet she felt no wrong,
Oh Love! how perfect is thy mystic art,
    Strengthening the weak, and trampling on the strong!
How self-deceitful is the sagest part
    Of mortals whom thy lure hath led along!—
The precipice she stood on was immense,
So was her creed in her own innocence.

She thought of her own strength, and Juan's youth,
    And of the folly of all prudish fears,   850
Victorious virtue, and domestic truth,
    And then of Don Alfonso's fifty years:

I wish these last had not occurr'd, in sooth,
  Because that number rarely much endears,
And through all climes, the snowy and the sunny,
Sounds ill in love, whate'er it may in money.

When people say, 'I've told you *fifty* times,'
  They mean to scold, and very often do;
When poets say, 'I've written *fifty* rhymes,'
  They make you dread that they'll recite them too;   860
In gangs of *fifty*, thieves commit their crimes;
  At *fifty* love for love is rare, 'tis true,
But then, no doubt it equally as true is,
A good deal may be bought for *fifty* Louis.

Julia had honour, virtue, truth, and love
  For Don Alfonso; and she inly swore,
By all the vows below to powers above,
  She never would disgrace the ring she wore,
Nor leave a wish which wisdom might reprove;
  And while she ponder'd this, besides much more,   870
One hand on Juan's carelessly was thrown,
Quite by mistake—she thought it was her own;

Unconsciously she lean'd upon the other,
  Which play'd within the tangles of her hair;
And to contend with thoughts she could not smother
  She seem'd, by the distraction of her air.
'Twas surely very wrong in Juan's mother
  To leave together this imprudent pair,
She who for many years had watch'd her son so—
I'm very certain *mine* would not have done so.   880

171

CXI

The hand which still held Juan's, by degrees
   Gently, but palpably confirm'd its grasp,
As if it said, 'Detain me, if you please';
   Yet there's no doubt she only meant to clasp
His fingers with a pure Platonic squeeze;
   She would have shrunk as from a toad, or asp,
Had she imagined such a thing could rouse
A feeling dangerous to a prudent spouse.

CXII

I cannot know what Juan thought of this,
   But what he did, is much what you would do;   890
His young lip thank'd it with a grateful kiss,
   And then, abash'd at its own joy, withdrew
In deep despair, lest he had done amiss,—
   Love is so very timid when 'tis new:
She blush'd, and frown'd not, but she strove to speak,
And held her tongue, her voice was grown so weak.

CXIII

The sun set, and up rose the yellow moon:
   The devil's in the moon for mischief; they
Who call'd her CHASTE, methinks, began too soon
   Their nomenclature; there is not a day,   900
The longest, not the twenty-first of June,
   Sees half the business in a wicked way,
On which three single hours of moonshine smile—
And then she looks so modest all the while.

CXIV

There is a dangerous silence in that hour,
   A stillness, which leaves room for the full soul
To open all itself, without the power
   Of calling wholly back its self-control;

The silver light which, hallowing tree and tower,
　　Sheds beauty and deep softness o'er the whole,　　910
Breathes also to the heart, and o'er it throws
A loving languor, which is not repose.

CXV

And Julia sate with Juan, half embraced
　　And half retiring from the glowing arm,
Which trembled like the bosom where 'twas placed;
　　Yet still she must have thought there was no harm,
Or else 'twere easy to withdraw her waist;
　　But then the situation had its charm,
And then——God knows what next—I can't go on;
I'm almost sorry that I e'er begun.　　920

CXVI

Oh Plato! Plato! you have paved the way,
　　With your confounded fantasies, to more
Immoral conduct by the fancied sway
　　Your system feigns o'er the controlless core
Of human hearts, than all the long array
　　Of poets and romancers:—You're a bore,
A charlatan, a coxcomb—and have been,
At best, no better than a go-between.

CXVII

And Julia's voice was lost, except in sighs,
　　Until too late for useful conversation;　　930
The tears were gushing from her gentle eyes,
　　I wish, indeed, they had not had occasion;
But who, alas! can love, and then be wise?
　　Not that remorse did not oppose temptation;
A little still she strove, and much repented,
And whispering 'I will ne'er consent'—consented.

'Tis said that Xerxes offer'd a reward
  To those who could invent him a new pleasure.
Methinks the requisition's rather hard,
  And must have cost his majesty a treasure: 940
For my part, I'm a moderate-minded bard,
  Fond of a little love (which I call leisure);
I care not for new pleasures, as the old
Are quite enough for me, so they but hold.

CXIX

Oh Pleasure! you're indeed a pleasant thing,
  Although one must be damn'd for you, no doubt:
I make a resolution every spring
  Of reformation ere the year run out,
But somehow, this my vestal vow takes wing,
  Yet still, I trust, it may be kept throughout: 950
I'm very sorry, very much ashamed,
And mean, next winter, to be quite reclaim'd.

CXX

Here my chaste Muse a liberty must take—
  Start not! still chaster reader—she'll be nice hence-
Forward, and there is no great cause to quake;
  This liberty is a poetic licence,
Which some irregularity may make
  In the design, and as I have a high sense
Of Aristotle and the Rules, 'tis fit
To beg his pardon when I err a bit.   960

CXXI

This licence is to hope the reader will
  Suppose from June the sixth (the fatal day
Without whose epoch my poetic skill
  For want of facts would all be thrown away),

174

But keeping Julia and Don Juan still
  In sight, that several months have pass'd; we'll say
'Twas in November, but I'm not so sure
About the day—the era's more obscure.

CXXII

We'll talk of that anon.—'Tis sweet to hear
  At midnight on the blue and moonlit deep   970
The song and oar of Adria's gondolier,
  By distance mellow'd, o'er the waters sweep;
'Tis sweet to see the evening star appear;
  'Tis sweet to listen as the night-winds creep
From leaf to leaf; 'tis sweet to view on high
The rainbow, based on ocean, span the sky.

CXXIII

'Tis sweet to hear the watch-dog's honest bark
  Bay deep-mouth'd welcome as we draw near home;
'Tis sweet to know there is an eye will mark
  Our coming, and look brighter when we come;   980
'Tis sweet to be awaken'd by the lark,
  Or lull'd by falling waters; sweet the hum
Of bees, the voice of girls, the song of birds,
The lisp of children, and their earliest words.

CXXIV

Sweet is the vintage, when the showering grapes
  In Bacchanal profusion reel to earth,
Purple and gushing; sweet are our escapes
  From civic revelry to rural mirth;
Sweet to the miser are his glittering heaps,
  Sweet to the father is his first-born's birth,   990
Sweet is revenge—especially to women,
Pillage to soldiers, prize-money to seamen.

175

CXXV

Sweet is a legacy, and passing sweet
  The unexpected death of some old lady
Or gentleman of seventy years complete,
  Who've made 'us youth' wait too—too long already
For an estate, or cash, or country seat,
  Still breaking, but with stamina so steady
That all the Israelites are fit to mob its
Next owner for their double-damn'd post-obits.   1000

CXXVI

'Tis sweet to win, no matter how, one's laurels,
  By blood or ink; 'tis sweet to out an end
To strife; 'tis sometimes sweet to have our quarrels,
  Particularly with a tiresome friend:
Sweet is old wine in bottles, ale in barrels;
  Dear is the helpless creature we defend
Against the world; and dear the schoolboy spot
We ne'er forget, though there we are forgot.

CXXVII

But sweeter still than this, than these, than all,
  Is first and passionate love—it stands alone,   1010
Like Adam's recollection of his fall;
  The tree of knowledge has been pluck'd—all's known—
And life yields nothing further to recall
  Worthy of this ambrosial sin, so shown,
No doubt in fable, as the unforgiven
Fire which Prometheus filch'd for us from heaven.

CXXVIII

Man's a strange animal, and makes strange use
  Of his own nature, and the various arts,
And likes particularly to produce
  Some new experiment to show his parts,   1020

176

This is the age of oddities let loose,
    Where different talents find their different marts;
You'd best begin with truth, and when you've lost your
Labour, there's a sure market for imposture.

CXXIX

What opposite discoveries we have seen!
    (Signs of true genius, and of empty pockets.)
One makes new noses, one a guillotine,
    One breaks your bones, one sets them in their sockets;
But vaccination certainly has been
    A kind antithesis to Congreve's rockets;   1030
With which the Doctor paid off an old pox,
By borrowing a new one from an ox.

CXXX

Bread has been made (indifferent) from potatoes;
    And galvanism has set some corpses grinning,
But has not answer'd like the apparatus
    Of the Humane Society's beginning,
By which men are unsuffocated gratis:
    What wondrous new machines have late been spinning!
I said the small pox has gone out of late;
Perhaps it may be follow'd by the great.   1040

CXXXI

'Tis said the great came from America;
    Perhaps it may set out on its return,—
The population there so spreads, they say
    'Tis grown high time to thin it in its turn,
With war, or plague, or famine, any way,
    So that civilisation they may learn;
And which in ravage the more loathsome evil is—
Their real lues, or our pseudo-syphilis?

177

CXXXII

This is the patent age of new inventions
  For killing bodies, and for saving souls,　　　　1050
All propagated with the best intentions;
  Sir Humphry Davy's lantern, by which coals
Are safely mined for in the mode he mentions,
  Tombuctoo travels, voyages to the Poles,
Are ways to benefit mankind, as true,
Perhaps, as shooting them at Waterloo.

CXXXIII

Man's a phenomenon, one knows not what,
  And wonderful beyond all wondrous measure;
'Tis pity though, in this sublime world, that
  Pleasure's a sin, and sometimes sin's a pleasure;　　1060
Few mortals know what end they would be at,
  But whether glory, power, or love, or treasure,
The path is through perplexing ways, and when
The goal is gain'd, we die, you know—and then——

CXXXIV

What then?—I do not know, no more do you—
  And so good night.—Return we to our story:
'Twas in November, when fine days are few,
  And the far mountains wax a little hoary,
And clap a white cape on their mantles blue;
  And the sea dashes round the promontory,　　　　1070
And the loud breaker boils against the rock,
And sober suns must set at five o'clock.

CXXXV

'Twas, as the watchmen say, a cloudy night;
  No moon, no stars, the wind was low or loud
By gusts, and many a sparkling hearth was bright
  With the piled wood, round which the family crowd;

178

There's something cheerful in that sort of light,
    Even as a summer sky's without a cloud:
I'm fond of fire, and crickets, and all that,
A lobster salad, and champagne, and chat.   1080

CXXXVI

'Twas midnight—Donna Julia was in bed,
    Sleeping, most probably,—when at her door
Arose a clatter might awake the dead,
    If they had never been awoke before,
And that they have been so we all have read,
    And are to be so, at the least, once more;—
The door was fasten'd, but with voice and fist
First knocks were heard, then 'Madam—Madam—hist!

CXXXVII

'For God's sake, Madam—Madam—here's my master,
    With more than half the city at his back—   1090
Was ever heard of such a curst disaster!
    'Tis not my fault—I kept good watch—Alack!
Do pray undo the bolt a little faster—
    They're on the stair just now, and in a crack
Will all be here; perhaps he yet may fly—
Surely the window's not so *very* high!'

CXXXVIII

By this time Don Alfonso was arrived,
    With torches, friends, and servants in great number;
The major part of them had long been wived,
    And therefore paused not to disturb the slumber   1100
Of any wicked woman, who contrived
    By stealth her husband's temples to encumber:
Examples of this kind are so contagious,
Were *one* not punish'd, *all* would be outrageous.

CXXXIX

I can't tell how, or why, or what suspicion
  Could enter into Don Alfonso's head;
But for a cavalier of his condition
  It surely was exceedingly ill-bred,
Without a word of previous admonition,
  To hold a levee round his lady's bed,   1110
And summon lackeys, arm'd with fire and sword,
To prove himself the thing he most abhorr'd.

CXL

Poor Donna Julia! starting as from sleep
  (Mind—that I do not say—she had not slept),
Began at once to scream, and yawn, and weep;
  Her maid, Antonia, who was an adept,
Contrived to fling the bed-clothes in a heap,
  As if she had just now from out them crept:
I can't tell why she should take all this trouble
To prove her mistress had been sleeping double.   1120

CXLI

But Julia mistress, and Antonia maid,
  Appear'd like two poor harmless women, who
Of goblins, but still more of men afraid,
  Had thought one man might be deterr'd by two,
And therefore side by side were gently laid,
  Until the hours of absence should run through,
And truant husband should return, and say,
'My dear, I was the first who came away.'

CXLII

Now Julia found at length a voice, and cried,
  'In heaven's name, Don Alfonso, what d'ye mean?   1130
Has madness seized you? would that I had died
  Ere such a monster's victim I had been!

What may this midnight violence betide,
   A sudden fit of drunkenness or spleen?
Dare you suspect me, whom the thought would kill?
Search, then, the room!'—Alfonso said, 'I will.'

CXLIII

He search'd, *they* search'd, and rummaged everywhere,
   Closet and clothes-press, chest and window-seat,
And found much linen, lace, and several pair
   Of stockings, slippers, brushes, combs, complete,   1140
With other articles of ladies fair,
   To keep them beautiful, or leave them neat:
Arras they prick'd and curtains with their swords,
And wounded several shutters, and some boards.

CXLIV

Under the bed they search'd, and there they found—
   No matter what—it was not that they sought;
They open'd windows, gazing if the ground
   Had signs or footmarks, but the earth said nought;
And then they stared each other's faces round:
   'Tis odd, not one of all these seekers thought,   1150
And seems to me almost a sort of blunder,
Of looking *in* the bed as well as under.

CXLV

During this inquisition Julia's tongue
   Was not asleep—'Yes, search and search,' she cried,
'Insult on insult heap, and wrong on wrong!
   It was for this that I became a bride!
For this in silence I have suffer'd long
   A husband like Alfonso at my side;
But now I'll bear no more, nor here remain,
If there be law or lawyers in all Spain.   1160

181

'Yes, Don Alfonso! husband now no more,
  If ever you indeed deserved the name,
Is't worthy of your years?—you have threescore—
  Fifty, or sixty, it is all the same—
Is't wise or fitting, causeless to explore
  For facts against a virtuous woman's fame?
Ungrateful, perjured, barbarous Don Alfonso,
How dare you think your lady would go on so?

'Is it for this I have disdain'd to hold
  The common privileges of my sex?   1170
That I have chosen a confessor so old
  And deaf, that any other it would vex,
And never once he has had cause to scold,
  But found my very innocence perplex
So much, he always doubted I was married—
How sorry you will be when I've miscarried!

'Was it for this that no Cortejo e'er
  I yet have chosen from out the youth of Seville?
Is it for this I scarce went anywhere,
  Except to bull-fights, mass, play, rout, and revel?   1180
Is it for this, whate'er my suitors were,
  I favour'd none—nay, was almost uncivil?
Is it for this that General Count O'Reilly,
Who took Algiers, declares I used him vilely?

'Did not the Italian Musico Cazzani
  Sing at my heart six months at least in vain?
Did not his countryman, Count Corniani,
  Call me the only virtuous wife in Spain?

Were there not also Russians, English, many?
   The Count Strongstroganoff I put in pain,   1190
And Lord Mount Coffeehouse, the Irish peer,
Who kill'd himself for love (with wine) last year.

CL

'Have I not had two bishops at my feet?
   The Duke of Ichar, and Don Fernan Nunez?
And is it thus a faithful wife you treat?
   I wonder in what quarter now the moon is:
I praise your vast forbearance not to beat
   Me also, since the time so opportune is—
Oh, valiant man! with sword drawn and cock'd trigger,
Now, tell me, don't you cut a pretty figure?   1200

CLI

'Was it for this you took your sudden journey,
   Under pretence of business indispensable,
With that sublime of rascals your attorney,
   Whom I see standing there, and looking sensible
Of having play'd the fool? though both I spurn, he
   Deserves the worst, his conduct's less defensible,
Because, no doubt, 'twas for his dirty fee,
And not from any love to you nor me.

CLII

'If he comes here to take a deposition,
   By all means let the gentleman proceed;   1210
You've made the apartment in a fit condition:—
   There's pen and ink for you, sir, when you need—
Let everything be noted with precision,
   I would not you for nothing should be fee'd—
But as my maid's undrest, pray turn your spies out.'
'Oh!' sobb'd Antonia, 'I could tear their eyes out.'

183

'There is the closet, there the toilet, there
  The antechamber—search them under, over;
There is the sofa, there the great armchair,
  The chimney—which would really hold a lover.   1220
I wish to sleep, and beg you will take care
  And make no further noise, till you discover
The secret cavern of this lurking treasure—
And when 'tis found, let me, too, have that pleasure.

CLIV

'And now, Hidalgo! now that you have thrown
  Doubt upon me, confusion over all,
Pray have the courtesy to make it known
  Who is the man you search for? how d'ye call
Him? what's his lineage? let him but be shown—
  I hope he's young and handsome—is he tall?   1230
Tell me—and be assured, that since you stain
Mine honour thus, it shall not be in vain.

CLV

'At least, perhaps, he has not sixty years,
  At that age he would be too old for slaughter,
Or for so young a husband's jealous fears—
  (Antonia! let me have a glass of water.)
I am ashamed of having shed these tears,
  They are unworthy of my father's daughter;
My mother dream'd not in my natal hour,
That I should fall into a monster's power.   1240

CLVI

'Perhaps 'tis of Antonia you are jealous,
  You saw that she was sleeping by my side,
When you broke in upon us with your fellows;
  Look where you please—we've nothing, sir, to hide;

Only another time, I trust, you'll tell us,
   Or for the sake of decency abide
A moment at the door, that we may be
Drest to receive so much good company.

CLVII

'And now, sir, I have done, and say no more;
   The little I have said may serve to show   1250
The guileless heart in silence may grieve o'er
   The wrongs to whose exposure it is slow:—
I leave you to your conscience as before,
   'Twill one day ask you, *why* you used me so?
God grant you feel not then the bitterest grief!
Antonia! where's my pocket-handkerchief?'

CLVIII

She ceased, and turn'd upon her pillow; pale
   She lay, her dark eyes flashing through their tears,
Like skies that rain and lighten; as a veil,
   Waved and o'ershading her wan cheek, appears   1260
Her streaming hair; the black curls strive, but fail,
   To hide the glossy shoulder, which uprears
Its snow through all;—her soft lips lie apart,
And louder than her breathing beats her heart.

CLIX

The Senhor Don Alfonso stood confused;
   Antonia bustled round the ransack'd room,
And, turning up her nose, with looks abused
   Her master, and his myrmidons, of whom
Not one, except the attorney, was amused;
   He, like Achates, faithful to the tomb,   1270
So there were quarrels, cared not for the cause,
Knowing they must be settled by the laws.

185

With prying snub-nose, and small eyes, he stood,
  Following Antonia's motions here and there,
With much suspicion in his attitude;
  For reputations he had little care;
So that a suit or action were made good,
  Small pity had he for the young and fair,
And ne'er believed in negatives, till these
Were proved by competent false witnesses.   1280

CLXI

But Don Alfonso stood with downcast looks,
  And, truth to say, he made a foolish figure;
When, after searching in five hundred nooks,
  And treating a young wife with so much rigour,
He gain'd no point, except some self-rebukes,
  Added to those his lady with such vigour
Had pour'd upon him for the last half hour,
Quick, thick, and heavy—as a thunder-shower.

CLXII

At first he tried to hammer an excuse,
  To which the sole reply was tears and sobs,   1290
And indications of hysterics, whose
  Prologue is always certain throes, and throbs,
Gasps, and whatever else the owners choose:
  Alfonso saw his wife, and thought of Job's;
He saw too, in perspective, her relations,
And then he tried to muster all his patience.

CLXIII

He stood in act to speak, or rather stammer,
  But sage Antonia cut him short before
The anvil of his speech received the hammer,
  With 'Pray, sir, leave the room, and say no more,   1300

Or madam dies.'—Alfonso mutter'd, 'D—n her,'
  But nothing else, the time of words was o'er;
He cast a rueful look or two, and did,
  He knew not wherefore, that which he was bid.

CLXIV

With him retired his '*posse comitatus,*'
  The attorney last, who linger'd near the door
Reluctantly, still tarrying there as late as
  Antonia let him—not a little sore
At this most strange and unexplain'd '*hiatus*'
  In Don Alfonso's facts, which just now wore   1310
An awkward look; as he revolved the case,
The door was fasten'd in his legal face.

CLXV

No sooner was it bolted, than—Oh shame!
  Oh sin! Oh sorrow! and Oh woman-kind!
How can you do such things and keep your fame,
  Unless this world, and t'other too, be blind?
Nothing so dear as an unfilch'd good name!
  But to proceed—for there is more behind:
With much heartfelt reluctance be it said,
Young Juan slipp'd, half-smother'd, from the bed.   1320

CLXVI

He had been hid—I don't pretend to say
  How, nor can I indeed describe the where—
Young, slender, and pack'd easily, he lay,
  No doubt, in little compass, round or square;
But pity him I neither must nor may
  His suffocation by that pretty pair;
'Twere better, sure, to die so, than be shut
With maudlin Clarence in his Malmsey butt.

And, secondly, I pity not, because
  He had no business to commit a sin,   1330
Forbid by heavenly, fined by human laws;
  At least 'twas rather early to begin;
But at sixteen the conscience rarely gnaws
  So much as when we call our old debts in
At sixty years, and draw the accompts of evil,
And find a deuced balance with the devil.

CLXVIII

Of his position I can give no notion:
  'Tis written in the Hebrew Chronicle,
How the physicians, leaving pill and potion,
  Prescribed, by way of blister, a young belle,   1340
When old King David's blood grew dull in motion,
  And that the medicine answer'd very well;
Perhaps 'twas in a different way applied,
For David lived, but Juan nearly died.

CLXIX

What's to be done? Alfonso will be back
  The moment he has sent his fools away.
Antonia's skill was put upon the rack,
  But no device could be brought into play—
And how to parry the renew'd attack?
  Besides, it wanted but few hours of day: 1350
Antonia puzzled; Julia did not speak,
But press'd her bloodless lip to Juan's cheek.

CLXX

He turn'd his lip to hers, and with his hand
  Call'd back the tangles of her wandering hair;
Even then their love they could not all command,
  And half forgot their danger and despair:

188

Antonia's patience now was at a stand—
    'Come, come, 'tis no time now for fooling there,'
She whisper'd, in great wrath—'I must deposit
This pretty gentleman within the closet: 1360

CLXXI

'Pray, keep your nonsense for some luckier night—
    Who can have put my master in this mood?
What will become on't—I'm in such a fright,
    The devil's in the urchin, and no good—
Is this a time for giggling? this a plight?
    Why, don't you know that it may end in blood?
You'll lose your life, and I shall lose my place,
My mistress all, for that half-girlish face.

CLXXII

'Had it but been for a stout cavalier
    Of twenty-five or thirty—(come, make haste)   1370
But for a child, what piece of work is here!
    I really, madam, wonder at your taste—
(Come, sir, get in)—my master must be near:
    There, for the present, at the least, he's fast,
And if we can but till the morning keep
Our counsel—(Juan, mind, you must not sleep).'

CLXXIII

Now, Don Alfonso entering, but alone,
    Closed the oration of the trusty maid:
She loiter'd, and he told her to be gone,
    An order somewhat sullenly obey'd;   1380
However, present remedy was none,
    And no great good seem'd answer'd if she staid;
Regarding both with slow and sidelong view,
She snuff'd the candle, curtsied, and withdrew.

Alfonso paused a minute—then begun
   Some strange excuses for his late proceeding:
He would not justify what he had done,
   To say the best, it was extreme ill-breeding;
But there were ample reasons for it, none
   Of which he specified in this his pleading: 1390
His speech was a fine sample, on the whole,
Of rhetoric, which the learn'd call '*rigmarole*.'

CLXXV

Julia said nought; though all the while there rose
   A ready answer, which at once enables
A matron, who her husband's foible knows,
   By a few timely words to turn the tables,
Which, if it does not silence, still must pose,—
   Even if it should comprise a pack of fables;
'Tis to retort with firmness, and when he
Suspects with *one*, do you reproach with *three*.   1400

CLXXVI

Julia, in fact, had tolerable grounds,—
   Alfonso's loves with Inez were well known;
But whether 'twas that one's own guilt confounds—
   But that can't be, as has been often shown,
A lady with apologies abounds;—
   It might be that her silence sprang alone
From delicacy to Don Juan's ear,
To whom she knew his mother's fame was dear.

CLXXVII

There might be one more motive, which makes two,
   Alfonso ne'er to Juan had alluded,—   1410
Mentioned his jealousy, but never who
   Had been the happy lover, he concluded,

Conceal'd amongst his premises; 'tis true,
   His mind the more o'er this its mystery brooded
To speak of Inez now were, one may say,
Like throwing Juan in Alfonso's way.

CLXXVIII

A hint, in tender cases, is enough;
   Silence is best: besides there is a *tact*—
(That modern phrase appears to me sad stuff,
   But it will serve to keep my verse compact)—   1420
Which keeps, when push'd by questions rather rough,
   A lady always distant from the fact:
The charming creatures lie with such a grace,
There's nothing so becoming to the face.

CLXXIX

They blush, and we believe them, at least I
   Have always done so; 'tis of no great use,
In any case, attempting a reply,
   For then their eloquence grows quite profuse;
And when at length they're out of breath, they sigh,
   And cast their languid eyes down, and let loose   1430
A tear or two, and then we make it up;
And then—and then—and then—sit down and sup.

CLXXX

Alfonso closed his speech, and begg'd her pardon,
   Which Julia half withheld, and then half granted,
And laid conditions, he thought very hard, on,
   Denying several little things he wanted:
He stood like Adam lingering near his garden,
   With useless penitence perplex'd and haunted,
Beseeching she no further would refuse,
When, lo! he stumbled o'er a pair of shoes.   1440

191

CLXXXI

A pair of shoes!—what then? not much, if they
    Are such as fit with ladies' feet, but these
(No one can tell how much I grieve to say)
    Were masculine; to see them, and to seize,
Was but a moment's act.—Ah! well-a-day!
    My teeth begin to chatter, my veins freeze—
Alfonso first examined well their fashion,
And then flew out into another passion.

CLXXXII

He left the room for his relinquish'd sword,
    And Julia instant to the closet flew.   1450
'Fly, Juan, fly! for heaven's sake—not a word—
    The door is open—you may yet slip through
The passage you so often have explored—
    Here is the garden-key—Fly—fly—Adieu!
Haste—haste! I hear Alfonso's hurrying feet—
Day has not broke—there's no one in the street.'

CLXXXIII

None can say that this was not good advice,
    The only mischief was, it came too late;
Of all experience 'tis the usual price,
    A sort of income-tax laid on by fate: 1460
Juan had reach'd the room-door in a trice,
    And might have done so by the garden-gate,
But met Alfonso in his dressing-gown,
Who threaten'd death—so Juan knock'd him down.

CLXXXIV

Dire was the scuffle, and out went the light;
    Antonia cried'out 'Rape!' and Julia 'Fire!'
But not a servant stirr'd to aid the fight.
    Alfonso, pommell'd to his heart's desire,

Swore lustily he'd be revenged this night;
   And Juan, too, blasphemed an octave higher;   1470
His blood was up: though young, he was a Tartar,
And not at all disposed to prove a martyr.

CLXXXV

Alfonso's sword had dropp'd ere he could draw it,
   And they continued battling hand to hand,
For Juan very luckily ne'er saw it;
   His temper not being under great command,
If at that moment he had chanced to claw it,
   Alfonso's days had not been in the land
Much longer.—Think of husbands', lovers' lives!
And how ye may be doubly widows—wives!   1480

CLXXXVI

Alfonso grappled to detain the foe,
   And Juan throttled him to get away,
And blood ('twas from the nose) began to flow;
   At last, as they more faintly wrestling lay,
Juan contrived to give an awkward blow,
   And then his only garment quite gave way;
He fled, like Joseph, leaving it; but there,
I doubt, all likeness ends between the pair.

CLXXXVII

Lights came at length, and men, and maids, who found
   An awkward spectacle their eyes before;   1490
Antonia in hysterics, Julia swoon'd,
   Alfonso leaning, breathless, by the door;
Some half-torn drapery scatter'd on the ground,
   Some blood, and several footsteps, but no more:
Juan the gate gain'd, turn'd the key about,
And liking not the inside, lock'd the out.

193

Here ends this canto—Need I sing, or say,
    How Juan, naked, favour'd by the night,
Who favours what she should not, found his way,
    And reach'd his home in an unseemly plight?   1500
The pleasant scandal which arose next day,
    The nine days' wonder which was brought to light,
And how Alfonso sued for a divorce,
Were in the English newspapers, of course.

If you would like to see the whole proceedings,
    The depositions and the cause at full,
The names of all the witnesses, the pleadings
    Of counsel to nonsuit, or to annul,
There's more than one edition, and the readings
    Are various, but they none of them are dull;   1510
The best is that in short-hand ta'en by Gurney,
Who to Madrid on purpose made a journey.

But Donna Inez, to divert the train
    Of one of the most circulating scandals
That had for centuries been known in Spain,
    At least since the retirement of the Vandals,
First vow'd (and never had she vow'd in vain)
    To Virgin Mary several pounds of candles;
And then, by the advice of some old ladies,
She sent her son to be shipp'd off from Cadiz.   1520

She had resolved that he should travel through
    All European climes, by land or sea,
To mend his former morals, and get new,
    Especially in France and Italy

(At least this is the thing most people do).
  Julia was sent into a convent: she
Grieved, but, perhaps, her feelings may be better
Shown in the following copy of her Letter:—

CXCII

'They tell me 'tis decided you depart:
    'Tis wise—'tis well, but not the less a pain;   1530
I have no further claim on your young heart,
    Mine is the victim, and would be gain:
To love too much has been the only art
    I used;—I write in haste, and if a stain
Be on this sheet, 'tis not what it appears;
My eyeballs burn and throb, but have no tears.

CXCIII

'I loved, I love you, for this love have lost
    State, station, heaven, mankind's, my own esteem,
And yet cannot regret what it hath cost,
    So dear is still the memory of that dream;   1540
Yet, if I name my guilt, 'tis not to boast,
    None can deem harshlier of me than I deem:
I trace this scrawl because I cannot rest—
I've nothing to reproach or to request.

CXCIV

'Man's love is of man's life a thing apart,
    'Tis woman's whole existence; man may range
The court, camp, church, the vessel, and the mart;
    Sword, gown, gain, glory, offer in exchange
Pride, fame, ambition, to fill up his heart,
    And few there are whom these cannot estrange;   1550
Men have all these resources, we but one,
To love again, and be again undone.

CXCV

'You will proceed in pleasure, and in pride,
　Beloved and loving many; all is o'er
For me on earth, except some years to hide
　My shame and sorrow deep in my heart's core:
These I could bear, but cannot cast aside
　The passion which still rages as before,—
And so farewell—forgive me, love me—No,
That word is idle now—but let it go.　　　　　　1560

CXCVI

'My breast has been all weakness, is so yet;
　But still I think I can collect my mind;
My blood still rushes where my spirit's set,
　As roll the waves before the settled wind;
My heart is feminine, nor can forget—
　To all, except one image, madly blind;
So shakes the needle, and so stands the pole,
As vibrates my fond heart to my fix'd soul.

CXCVII

'I have no more to say, but linger still,
　And dare not set my seal upon this sheet,　　　　1570
And yet I may as well the task fulfil.
　My misery can scarce be more complete:
I had not lived till now, could sorrow kill;
　Death shuns the wretch who fain the blow would meet,
And I must even survive this last adieu,
And bear with life to love and pray for you!'

CXCVIII

This note was written upon gilt-edged paper
　With a neat little crow-quill, slight and new;
Her small white hand could hardly reach the taper,
　It trembled as magnetic needles do,　　　　　　1580

And yet she did not let one tear escape her;
  The seal a sun-flower; '*Elle vous suit partout,*'
The motto, cut upon a white cornelian;
The wax was superfine, its hue vermilion.

CXCIX

This was Don Juan's earliest scrape; but whether
  I shall proceed with his adventures is
Dependent on the public altogether;
  We'll see, however, what they say to this,
Their favour in an author's cap's a feather,
  And no great mischief's done by their caprice;   1590
And if their approbation we experience,
Perhaps they'll have some more about a year hence.

CC

My poem's epic, and is meant to be
  Divided in twelve books; each book containing,
With love, and war, a heavy gale at sea,
  A list of ships, and captains, and kings reigning,
New characters; the episodes are three:
  A panoramic view of hell's in training,
After the style of Virgil and of Homer,
So that my name of Epic's no misnomer.   1600

CCI

All these things will be specified in time,
  With strict regard to Aristotle's rules,
The *Vade Mecum* of the true sublime,
  Which makes so many poets, and some fools:
Prose poets like blank-verse, I'm fond of rhyme,
  Good workmen never quarrel with their tools;
I've got new mythological machinery,
And very handsome supernatural scenery.

197

There's only one slight difference between
   Me and my epic brethren gone before,   1610
And here the advantage is my own, I ween
   (Not that I have not several merits more,
But this will more peculiarly be seen);
   They so embellish, that 'tis quite a bore
Their labyrinth of fables to thread through,
Whereas this story's actually true.

If any person doubt it, I appeal
   To history, tradition, and to facts,
To newspapers, whose truth all know and feel,
   To plays in five, and operas in three acts;   1620
All these confirm my statement a good deal,
   But that which more completely faith exacts
Is, that myself, and several now in Seville,
Saw Juan's last elopement with the devil.

If ever I should condescend to prose,
   I'll write poetical commandments, which
Shall supersede beyond all doubt all those
   That went before; in these I shall enrich
My text with many things that no one knows,
   And carry precept to the highest pitch: 1630
I'll call the work 'Longinus o'er a Bottle,
Or, Every Poet his *own* Aristotle.'

Thou shalt believe in Milton, Dryden, Pope;
   Thou shalt not set up Wordsworth, Coleridge, Southey;
Because the first is crazed beyond all hope,
   The second drunk, the third so quaint and mouthy:

With Crabbe it may be difficult to cope,
   And Campbell's Hippocrene is somewhat drouthy:
Thou shalt not steal from Samuel Rogers, nor
Commit—flirtation with the muse of Moore.   1640

CCVI

Thou shalt not covet Mr. Sotheby's Muse,
   His Pegasus, nor anything that's his;
Thou shalt not bear false witness like 'the Blues'—
   (There's *one*, at least is very fond of this);
Thou shalt not write, in short, but what I choose;
   This is true criticism, and you may kiss—
Exactly as you please, or not,—the rod;
But if you don't, I'll lay it on, by G—d!

CCVII

If any person should presume to assert
   This story is not moral, first, I pray,   1650
That they will not cry out before they're hurt,
   Then that they'll read it o'er again, and say
(But, doubtless, nobody will be so pert),
   That this is not a moral tale, though gay;
Besides, in Canto Twelfth, I mean to show
The very place where wicked people go.

CCVIII

If, after all, there should be some so blind
   To their own good this warning to despise,
Let by some tortuosity of mind,
   Not to believe my verse and their own eyes,   1660
And cry that they 'the moral cannot find,'
   I tell him, if a clergyman, he lies;
Should captains the remark, or critics, make,
They also lie too—under a mistake.

The public approbation I expect,
   And beg they'll take my word about the moral,
Which I with their amusement will connect
   (So children cutting teeth receive a coral);
Meantime they'll doubtless please to recollect
   My epical pretensions to the laurel: 1670
For fear some prudish readers should grow skittish,
I've bribed my Grandmother's Review—the British.

I sent it in a letter to the Editor,
   Who thank'd me duly by return of post—
I'm for a handsome article his creditor;
   Yet, if my gentle Muse he please to roast,
And break a promise after having made it her,
   Denying the receipt of what it cost,
And smear his page with gall instead of honey,
All I can say is—that he had the money.   1680

I think that with this holy new alliance
   I may ensure the public, and defy
All other magazines of art or science,
   Daily, or monthly, or three monthly; I
Have not essay'd to multiply their clients,
   Because they tell me 'twere in vain to try,
And that the Edinburgh Review and Quarterly
Treat a dissenting author very martyrly.

'*Non ego hoc ferrem calida juventa*
   Consule Planco,' Horace said, and so   1690
Say I; by which quotation there is meant a
   Hint that some six or seven good years ago

(Long ere I dreamt of dating from the Brenta)
   I was most ready to return a blow,
And would not brook at all this sort of thing
In my hot youth—when George the Third was King.

CCXIII

But now at thirty years my hair is gray—
   (I wonder what it will be like at forty?
I thought of a peruke the other day—)
   My heart is not much greener; and, in short, I   1700
Have squander'd my whole summer while 'twas May,
   And feel no more the spirit to retort; I
Have spent my life, both interest and principal,
And deem not, what I deem'd, my soul invincible.

CCXIV

No more—no more—Oh! never more on me
   The freshness of the heart can fall like dew,
Which out of all the lovely things we see
   Extracts emotions beautiful and new;
Hived in our bosoms like the bag o' the bee.
   Think'st thou the honey with those objects grew?   1710
Alas! 'twas not in them, but in thy power
To double even the sweetness of a flower.

CCXV

No more—no more—Oh! never more, my heart,
   Canst thou be my sole world, my universe!
Once all in all, but now a thing apart,
   Thou canst not be my blessing or my curse:
The illusion's gone for ever, and thou art
   Insensible, I trust, but none the worse,
And in thy stead I've got a deal of judgment,
Though heaven knows how it ever found a lodgment.   1720

201

My days of love are over; me no more
 The charms of maid, wife, and still less of widow,
Can make the fool of which they made before,—
 In short, I must not lead the life I did do;
The credulous hope of mutual minds is o'er,
 The copious use of claret is forbid too,
So for a good old-gentlemanly vice,
I think I must take up with avarice.

Ambition was my idol, which was broken
 Before the shrines of Sorrow, and of Pleasure;   1730
And the two last have left me many a token
 O'er which reflection may be made at leisure;
Now, like Friar Bacon's brazen head, I've spoken,
 'Time is, Time was, Time's past':—a chymic treasure
Is glittering youth, which I have spent betimes—
My heart in passion, and my head on rhymes.

What is the end of fame? 'tis but to fill
 A certain portion of uncertain paper:
Some liken it to climbing up a hill,
 Whose summit, like all hills, is lost in vapour;   1740
For this men write, speak, preach, and heroes kill,
 And bards burn what they call their 'midnight taper,'
To have, when the original is dust,
A name, a wretched picture, and worse bust.

What are the hopes of man? Old Egypt's King
 Cheops erected the first pyramid
And largest, thinking it was just the thing
 To keep his memory whole, and mummy hid:

But somebody or other rummaging,
   Burglariously broke his coffin's lid: 1750
Let not a monument give you or me hopes,
Since not a pinch of dust remains of Cheops.

CCXX

But I, being fond of true philosophy,
   Say very often to myself, 'Alas!
All things that have been born were born to die,
   And flesh (which Death mows down to hay) is grass;
You've pass'd your youth not so unpleasantly,
   And if you had it o'er again—'twould pass—
So thank your stars that matters are no worse,
And read your Bible, sir, and mind your purse.'   1760

CCXXI

But for the present, gentle reader! and
   Still gentler purchaser! the bard—that's I—
Must, with permission, shake you by the hand,
   And so your humble servant, and goodbye!
We meet again, if we should understand
   Each other; and if not, I shall not try
Your patience further than by this short sample—
'Twere well if others follow'd my example.

CCXXII

'Go, little book, from this my solitude!
   I cast thee on the waters—go thy ways!   1770
And if, as I believe, thy vein be good,
   The world will find thee after many days.'
When Southey's read, and Wordsworth understood,
   I can't help putting in my claim to praise—
The four first rhymes are Southey's, every line:
For God's sake, reader! take them not for mine!

203

NOTES

17. FROM ANACREON

Anacreon, the Greek Lyric poet, was born at Teos in Asia Minor about 550 B.C. He died aged eighty-five in Athens. Most of the work that bears his name is, in fact, that of later imitators. His lyrics have been translated or imitated by many English poets from the seventeenth century onwards.

l.3. Boötes: the stellar constellation now known as The Great Bear.

l.7. Paphian Boy: Cupid, or Eros, the boy God of Love, was the son of Aphrodite who was born out of the foam on the shores of Paphos.

20. WRITTEN AFTER SWIMMING FROM SESTOS TO ABYDOS

Byron accomplished the feat of swimming the Hellespont on May 3, 1810, together with Lieutenant Ekenhead of the frigate *Salsette*. The swim, which was one of over four miles, took just over an hour.

The story of Hero and Leander is, briefly: Leander was in love with Hero, the priestess of Aphrodite, and, in order to visit her, swam the Hellespont to Sestos every night. One night, on his return journey to Abydos, he was drowned, and Hero threw herself into the sea in her grief.

21. TO BELSHAZZAR

See *The Book of Daniel*, Chapter 5.

22. TO THOMAS MOORE

Thomas Moore, the poet and song writer, was one of Byron's closest friends. He was born in 1779 and died in 1852.

24. FOUR EPIGRAMS

l.5. Castlereagh: In August 1820 the then Foreign Secretary, Robert Stewart, Viscount Castlereagh, and 2nd Marquis of Londonderry, getting suddenly out of bed, where he had been ill of a fever, cut his throat. He was much hated by the radical politicians of the period who, in fact, called him 'carotid-artery-cutting Castlereagh', largely because of his economic policies which appeared to them to be responsible for much of the unemployment and consequent starvation of the working classes in this period.

29. ONE STRUGGLE MORE, AND I AM FREE

l.29. at Cynthia's noon: Cynthia being a term for the moon, this phrase means 'At the full moon'.

31. THE DESTRUCTION OF SENNACHERIB
See *The Second Book of Kings*, Chapter 19.

32. *From* THE CORSAIR
Conrad, the Corsair, returning to his beloved Medora after many bloody adventures, finds her dead. The lines

> 'His heart was form'd for softness—warped to wrong;
> Betray'd too early, and beguiled too long'

have often been regarded as autobiographical reflections.

37. IF SOMETIMES IN THE HAUNTS OF MEN
l.20. a Lethe for despair: Lethe is the river in the Underworld from which the spirits of the dead drink in order to forget the past; it is therefore often used as a synonym for Forgetfulness.

38. *From* THE ISLAND
This poem is based upon the well-known story of the mutiny on the *Bounty*, and describes the mutineers after the fight.

43. STANZAS TO AUGUSTA
Augusta is, of course, Byron's half-sister, Augusta Leigh.

49. *From* CHILDE HAROLD'S PILGRIMAGE
Childe Harold's Pilgrimage was published in three parts; the first, of two cantos, appeared in 1812; the third canto followed in 1816, and the fourth, and last, canto was published in 1818. The poem is a description of the journeys and reflections of the hero, a lonely, gloomy, embittered and passionate man. In the fourth canto the fictional pilgrim is almost entirely forgotten and Byron speaks out in his own person. Byron himself explained the reason for this change in a preface to the fourth canto, which he addressed to Hobhouse:

'The fact is, that I had become weary of drawing a line which everyone seemed determined not to perceive: like the Chinese in Goldsmith's *Citizen of the World*, whom nobody would believe to be a Chinese, it was in vain that I asserted, and imagined that I had drawn, a distinction between the author and the pilgrim; and the very anxiety to preserve this difference, and disappointment at finding it unavailing, so far crushed my efforts in the composition, that I determined to abandon it altogether—and have done so.'

XCVI. *Columbia:* America. *Pallas:* Pallas Athene who sprang fully armed from the head of Zeus, her father. She was the Goddess of the intellect, and also a Goddess of war. *Washington:* George Washington (1732–1799), the first President of the U.S.A.

XCVII. *Saturnalia:* this was a Roman Festival in honour of the God Saturn. It began on December 17 and lasted seven days, and was a time of great revelry.

CXXVI. *upas:* the juice of the upas tree is supposed to be used to envenom the darts of the natives of Java. It has also been said that the tree is so poisonous that it kills all animal life within a radius of fifteen miles.

CXXXII. *Nemesis:* a Greek Goddess who gave to mortals their allotted amounts of happiness and misery, and who made the over-wealthy suffer loss and pain. She is also regarded as the goddess who saw to it that all crimes were punished sooner or later. *Orestes* was the son of Agamemnon and Clytemnestra. He killed his mother because she had murdered his father, and was thereafter pursued by the Furies.

59. THE SIEGE OF CORINTH

Byron printed the following quotation as a preface to this poem:

'The grand army of the Turks (in 1715), under the Prime Vizier, to open to themselves a way into the heart of the Morea, and to form the siege of Napoli di Romania, the most considerable place in all that country, thought it best in the first place to attack Corinth, upon which they made several storms. The garrison being weakened, and the governor seeing it was impossible to hold out against so mighty a force, thought it fit to beat a parley: but while they were treating about the articles, one of the magazines in the Turkish camp, wherein they had six hundred barrels of powder, blew up by accident, whereby six or seven hundred men were killed; which so enraged the infidels, that they would not grant any capitulation, but stormed the place with so much fury, that they took it, and put most of the garrison, with Signior Minotti, the governor, to the sword. The rest, with Antonio Bembo, proveditor extraordinary, were made prisoners of war.' *History of the Turks*, vol iii, p. 151.

*l.*10. *capote:* a long outer garment made of rough cloth or skins with the hair still on, which was worn in the Levant by members of both sexes.

*l.*98. *Othman's sons:* Othman, or Osman, the First founded the Ottoman Empire and the Osman line of Sultans in about A.D. 1300.

*l.*133. *Lion's Mouth:* the mouth of one of the stone lions of St. Marks, Venice, into which dissatisfied citizens could place petitions and complaints.

*l.*141. *Coumourgi:* Ali Coumourgi, the favourite of three Sultans, and Grand Vizier to Achmet III, after recovering Peloponnesus from the Venetians in one campaign, was mortally wounded in the next, against the Germans, at the battle of Peterwardin (in the plain of Carlowitz), in Hungary, endeavouring to rally his guards. He died of his wounds next day. His last order was the decapitation of General Breuner and some other German prisoners; and his last words, 'Oh that I could thus serve all the Christian dogs!' a speech and act not unlike one of Caligula. He was a young man of great ambition and unbounded presumption: on being told that Prince Eugene, then opposed to him, 'was a great general', he said, 'I shall become a greater, and at his expense'. (Byron's note.)

l.199. *Paynim*: Moslem.

l.225. *Menelaus* was the King of Sparta, whose wife, Helen, was stolen away by Paris, thus causing the Trojan War.

l.266. *Muezzin*: the man who calls the faithful to prayer in Moslem countries.

l.301. *Houris* are beautiful virgins who entertain devout Moslems when they reach Paradise.

l.469. *tuft of hair*: this tuft, or long lock, is left from a superstition that Mahomet will draw them into paradise by it. (Byron's note.)

l.688. *Horsetails*: the horsetail, fixed upon a lance, a Pacha's standard. (Byron's note.)

l.704. *Janizar*: a member of the force of Janissaries who, until 1826, constituted the standing army of the Ottoman Empire.

l.810. *Patroclus* was the friend of Achilles and accompanied him to the Trojan War. Achilles had decided not to fight any more, when the death of Patroclus at the hands of Hector made him change his mind. He returned to the battle and killed a great many Trojans in vengeance.

l.869. *falchion's point*: a falchion is a broad-bladed, slightly curved sword which was used in the Middle Ages.

92. THE PRISONER OF CHILLON

This poem is based upon the imprisonment of Francois de Bonnivard, the Genevan patriot, by the Duke of Savoy, for his attempts to preserve the freedom of the Genevan Republic. He was imprisoned in the Chateau de Chillon, which overlooked Lake Geneva, from 1530 to 1536, without ever being brought to trial.

104. THE VISION OF JUDGMENT

This poem, published pseudonymously over the name 'Quevedo Redivivus', was, in Byron's words, 'suggested by the composition so entitled by the author of *Wat Tyler*'. *Wat Tyler* was a poem by Southey that was stigmatized as blasphemous and seditious; the same author's *Vision of Judgment* was a pæan of praise for what we nowadays call The Establishment. Byron objected to Southey's change from radical republicanism to royalism, as he also objected to Southey's recommendation that the Legislature should look at the poetry of the so-called 'Satanic School'. He accused him of turning informer. He also pointed out that Southey, in praising Landor's poem

Gebir, was praising a work in which George the Fourth was attacked, even though Southey himself had made the King the 'hero' of his own heaven.

VII. *Saint John's foretold beast:* See *Book of Revelation.*

XII. *German will:* this is a play upon the word 'german' which can mean appropriate or relevant, or can refer to Germany, the country of the King's origin, and the country in which many of his relations lived.

XIX. *king of France:* Louis XVI (1754–1793).

XX. *Paul—the parvenu:* St. Paul was a late-comer to the ranks of Christ followers, but rose to a high position nevertheless.

XXVI. *Orion's Belt:* this is part of a constellation which is represented on pictorial charts as a man (Orion, the hunter), who is wearing a belt formed by three stars. *Tories:* a term descriptive of a group of English politicians who sought to maintain the extreme prerogatives of the crown, and who were in all respects very conservative.

XXVII. *Captain Parry's crew:* members of an early expedition to the Arctic under the leadership of Sir Edward Parry (1790–1855).

XXVIII. *Johanna Southcote*, or Southcott, was a religious fanatic, who left behind her a box which, when opened, would reveal many things. She was born in 1750, and died in 1814.

XXXII. *champ clos:* literally, an enclosed field. The equivalent English expression is 'stamping ground'.

XLIII. *to a minion:* the reference is to Lord Bute.

XLVI. *Apicius' board:* the table of a famous Roman epicure of the first century.

XLVIII. *the primitive:* Roman Catholics.

XLIX. *Guelph:* the Guelphs were a powerful aristocratic family of Italy and Germany from the ninth to the fifteenth century.

L. *Cerberus:* the many-headed dog that guards the entrance to Hades in Greek mythology. *Bedlam:* St. Mary of Bethlehem's Hospital, which was originally a religious house, and which became a Hospital for the Insane in 1547.

LII. *which Milton mentions:* See *Paradise Lost, Book Six.*

LXV. *Jack Wilkes:* the English political agitator (1727–1797).

LXXI. *Bute and Grafton:* the Earl of Bute (1713–1792) was a leader of the politicians supporting George III. The Duke of Grafton (1735–1811) was also a conservative politician.

LXXIII. *Fox's lard was basting William Pitt:* Charles James Fox (1749–1806) was the main antagonist of the Government of William Pitt (1759–1806), and the leader of the Whig, or Liberal, Party of his time.

LXXIV. *Junius:* the pseudonym of an unknown author who wrote a series of letters attacking the British Government in the years 1769–1772.

LXXIX. *Mrs. Malaprop:* a character in Sheridan's play, *The Rivals*, who was given to using long words in the wrong context, and betraying her ignorance where she wished to display her learning, cf., the French, *Mal à propos*. *Burke:* Edmund Burke (1729–1797), the statesman and orator. *Tooke:* John Horne Tooke (1726–1812) was a politician and philosopher. He opposed the war with America in 1776. *Sir Philip Francis:* (1740–1818) was a writer on politics. Some historians think he may have been the author of the *Letters of Junius* (see above).

LXXXIV. *Franklin:* Benjamin Franklin (1706–1790) was an American diplomat and wit.

LXXXIX. *Balaam's ass:* the ass which spoke in order to induce the prophet, its master, to bless rather than curse Israel.

XCII. *Pye:* Henry James Pye was Poet Laureate from 1790 to 1813. He was succeeded by Robert Southey.

XCIII. *Castlereagh:* i.e., Robert Stewart, Viscount Castlereagh (1769–1822). See p. 205.

XCIV. *poetic felony 'de se':* 'Felo de se' is the legal term for the criminal offence of committing suicide, or attempting self-destruction.

CI. *King Alfonso:* Alfonzo X, the King of Leon and Castile (1252–1282), was called both 'The Wise' and 'The Astronomer'.

CIV. *Phaeton:* the son of Helios, the Sun God. Allowed one day, after much pleading, to drive the sun chariot across the sky, he lost control of it and was killed by Jupiter, his body falling into the river Po.

CV. *buoy'd like corks:* a drowned body lies at the bottom till rotten; it then floats, as most people know. (Byron's note.)

135. DON JUAN: DEDICATION

VII. *Scott, Rogers, Campbell, Moore, and Crabbe·* these poets were all contemporaries of Byron. Their dates are: Sir Walter Scott, 1771–1832; Samuel Rogers, 1763–1855; Thomas Campbell, 1777–1844; Thomas Moore, 1779–1852; George Crabbe, 1754–1832.

IX. *Titan:* one of the primeval deities who were children of Uranus and Gaea in Greek mythology. They include Cronus and Rhea from whom were descended Zeus and the Olympians; the Titan Hyperion fathered the Sun god and sometimes this god was called Titan.

XI. *Like Samuel from the grave:* the Witch of Endor is supposed to have called Samuel up from the grave.

XII. *Erin's gore:* Erin means Ireland.

XIII. *Ixion:* in Greek mythology, a king of the Lapithae who was bound to an endlessly turning wheel as a punishment.

XVII. *'buff and blue':* the uniform of the Whig Club of Fox's time; hence, the buff and blue cover of the *Edinburgh Review*. (Byron's note.) *Ultra-Julian:* I allude not to our friend Landor's hero, the traitor Count Julian, but to Gibbon's hero, vulgarly yclept 'The Apostate'. (Byron's note.)

II. *Vernon . . . Cumberland, Wolfe, Hawke, Prince Ferdinand, Granby, Burgoyne, Keppel, Howe:* all Naval and Military leaders of the time. *Wellesley:* Arthur Wellesley, the first Duke of Wellington, the victor of Waterloo (1769–1852). *Buonaparté and Dumourier:* Buonaparte is, of course, the French Emperor Napoleon (1769–1821). Dumourier was a French general (1739–1823).

III. *Barnave, Brissot, Condorcet, Mirabeau, Pétion, Clootz, Danton, Marat, La Fayette:* leaders and leading thinkers of the French Revolution. *Joubert, Hoche, Marceau, Lannes, Desaix, Moreau:* French soldiers.

IV. *Duncan, Nelson, Howe, and Jervis:* British admirals.

V. *Agamemnon:* 'Vixere fortes ante *Agamemnona*, etc., Horace. (Byron's note.)

VI. *in medias res:* In the middle of things. *Horace:* Quintus Horatius Flaccus, the Latin poet who lived from 65 B.C. to A.D. 8.

IX. *Hidalgo:* a Spanish nobleman of minor distinction.

XI. *Calderon:* a Spanish dramatic poet (1562–1635). *Lopé:* i.e., Felix Lope de Vega (1562–1635), the Spanish poet and dramatist. *Feinagle's were an useless art:* Gregor von Feinagle (1765–1819) was the inventor of a system to aid the memory.

XII. *Attic:* simple, refined, pure, and elegant.

XV. *Sir Samuel Romilly:* English lawyer and statesman (1757–1818).

XVI. *Miss Edgeworth's novels:* Maria Edgeworth lived from 1767 to 1849 and was the author of many novels and didactic works. *Mrs. Trimmer's books on education:* a prolific and popular author of improving books, Sarah Trimmer lived from 1741 to 1810. *Coelebs' Wife:* the title of a novel by Hannah More published in 1809.

XVII. *Harrison:* John Harrison, the famous clockmaker, lived from 1693 to 1776. *Macassar:* 'Description des *vertus incomparables* de l'huile Macassar— See the Advertisement.' (Byron's note.) A widely used and very widely advertised hair dressing.

XXXV. *Numa's . . . Pompilius:* Pompilius Numa was the legendary second King of Rome, and noted for his wisdom and piety.

XXXVII. *messuages:* a legal term for dwelling houses and buildings and the land adjoining them.

XLII. *Ovid:* Publius Ovidius Naso, the Roman poet, lived from 43 B.C. to A.D. 17. *Anacreon:* See above. *Catullus:* Caius Valerios Catullus, the Roman poet, lived from 87 B.C. to 54 B.C. *Virgil:* Publius Virgilius Maro, the Roman poet and author of the *Aeneid*, lived from 70 B.C. to 19 B.C.

XLIII. *Lucretius:* Titus Lucretius Carus, the Roman poet, and author of *De Rerum Natura*, lived from 96 B.C. to 55 B.C. *Juvenal:* Decimus Junius Juvenalis was a Roman satirical poet who constantly attacked the vices of his time. His dates are unknown, but he flourished during the final years of the first century. *Martial:* Marcus Valerius Martialis was a Roman epigrammatist who lived, from, A.D. 40 to A.D. 104.

XLIV. *trouble of an index:* Fact. There is, or was, such an edition, with all the obnoxious epigrams of Martial placed by themselves at the end. (Byron's note.)

XLVII. *Jerome:* Saint Jerome (A.D. 340?–A.D. 420) was a Latin father of the Church. *Chrysostom:* Saint John Chrysostom (A.D. 347?–A.D. 407) was a Greek father of the Church. *Saint Augustine:* See his Confessions I. i. c. ix. By the representation which Saint Augustine gives of himself in his youth, it is easy to see that he was what we should call a rake. He avoided the school as the plague; he loved nothing but gaming and public shows; he robbed his father of everything he could find; he invented a thousand lies to escape the rod, which they were obliged to make use of to punish his irregularities. (Byron's note.)

LVI. *Boabdil:* Abu Abdallah (El Chico), the last Moorish King of Granada, who flourished around 1481.

LXII. *'mi vien in mente':* it comes to mind.

LXIV. *St. Anthony:* for particulars of St. Anthony's recipe for hot blood in cold weather, see Mr. Alban Butler's 'Lives of the Saints'. (Byron's note.)

LXXV. *Tarquin:* Lucius Tarquinius Superbus, otherwise called Tarquin the Proud, was the seventh and last legendary King of Rome.

LXXXVI. *Miss Medea:* Medea, daughter of the King of Colchis, fell in love with Jason who had come to Colchis to get the golden fleece and helped him to obtain it.

LXXXVIII. *a god indeed divine:* Campbell's *Gertrude of Wyoming*. I think the opening of Canto II, but quote from memory. (Byron's note.)

XCV. *Boscan or Garcillasso:* Spanish poets.

CIV. *Anacreon Moore:* one of Byron's names for his friend Thomas Moore.

CXVI. *Plato:* the Greek philosopher, lived from 427 B.C. to 347 B.C.

CXVIII. *Xerxes:* the great King of Persia from 486 B.C. to 465 B.C.

CXX. *Aristotle:* the Greek philosopher, lived from 384 B.C. to 322 B.C.

CXXIV. *Bacchanal:* refers to Bacchus the Greek god of wine, whose devotees were given to great revelries.

CXXVII. *Prometheus:* one of the Titans (see p. 210) stole fire from heaven to give to humanity. For this he was punished by Zeus, by being manacled to a rock where his liver was torn out by eagles each day, only to be renewed each night.

CXXIX. *Congreve's rockets:* Sir William Congreve (1772–1828), English engineer, was responsible for the invention of a rocket.

CXXX. *galvanism . . .* etc., electric shocks were given experimentally to corpses, causing muscular spasms.

CXXXII. *Sir Humphry Davy:* a chemist, the inventor of a miners' safety lamp (1778–1829).

CXLVIII. *Count O'Reilly:* Donna Julia has made a mistake. Count O'Reilly did not take Algiers, but Algiers very nearly took him: he and his army and fleet retreated with great loss, and not much credit, from before that city, in the year 1775. (Byron's note.)

CLIX. *Achates:* Achates was the faithful friend of Aeneas.

CCIV. *Longinus:* the Greek philosopher and critic, lived from A.D. 213 to A.D. 273. He is particularly noted for his work *On the Sublime.*

CCV. *Hippocrene:* a fountain which sprung from the earth at the stamp of the hoof of Pegasus, the winged horse of Greek mythology. Its waters are supposed to impart poetic inspiration.

CCVI. *Pegasus:* arose from the body of the Gorgon slain by Perseus and was later tamed by the hero, Bellerophon. It is associated with poetry and with the notion of poetic inspiration, and is regarded as the horse of the Muses.

CCIX. *coral:* once used as a teething ring for babies.

CCXVII. *Friar Bacon:* Roger Bacon, the philosopher (1214?–1294), had a great reputation as a magician. He is supposed to have made a brazen head which could foretell the future if it were asked the right question at the right time. Tired out with waiting for the head to speak and announce that the time had come to ask the question, Friar Bacon fell asleep, and only his apprentice heard the brazen head say 'Time is', then 'Time was', and, finally, 'Time's Past', whereupon the head was mysteriously destroyed. This legend is retold in the comedy *Friar Bacon and Friar Bungay* by Robert Greene (1558-1592).

CCXIX. *Cheops:* was the Egyptian king responsible for building the largest of the pyramids near Gizeh. He flourished about 3700 B.C.

INDEX OF FIRST LINES

215